The Literature of Cinema

ADVISORY EDITOR: **MARTIN S. DWORKIN**
INSTITUTE OF PHILOSOPHY AND POLITICS OF EDUCATION
TEACHER'S COLLEGE, COLUMBIA UNIVERSITY

THE LITERATURE OF CINEMA presents
a comprehensive selection from the multitude
of writings about cinema, rediscovering materials on its origins, history, theoretical principles and techniques, aesthetics, economics,
and effects on societies and individuals. Included are works of inherent, lasting merit
and others of primarily historical significance.
These provide essential resources for serious
study and critical enjoyment of the "magic
shadows" that became one of the decisive cul-
tural forces of modern times.

TWENTY YEARS
OF BRITISH FILM
1925–1945

MICHAEL BALCON

ERNEST LINDGREN

FORSYTH HARDY

ROGER MANVELL

ARNO PRESS & THE NEW YORK TIMES

NEW YORK • 1972

Reprint Edition 1972 by Arno Press Inc.

Reprinted from a copy in the Library of John P. Lowe
LC# 73-169326
ISBN 0-405-03890-9

The Literature of Cinema - Series II
ISBN for complete set: 0-405-03887-9
See last pages of this volume for titles.

Manufactured in the United States of America

TWENTY YEARS
OF BRITISH FILM
1925—1945

TWENTY YEARS

OF BRITISH FILM

1925–1945

MICHAEL BALCON

ERNEST LINDGREN

FORSYTH HARDY

ROGER MANVELL

THE FALCON PRESS LIMITED • 1947

First published in 1947
by the Falcon Press (London) Limited
7 Crown Passage, Pall Mall, London, S.W.1
Printed in Great Britain
by Dugdale Printing Limited
122 Wardour Street, London, W.1

7W-020749 -6

791.430941 (22)

CONTENTS

The publishers would like to thank the Central Office of Information, the National Film Library, the Edinburgh Film Guild, and the film companies who have allowed the reproduction of stills from their collections.

MICHAEL BALCON

THE BRITISH FILM TO-DAY

To the philosophers who believe that there is nothing new under the sun it is already apparent that the aftermath of one world war is little different from that of another. Since the thought is depressing and even disquieting it is consoling to reflect that there *are* differences in the smaller issues however these may be overshadowed (as they are at the time this article is being written) by larger considerations. For instance, nobody of my generation and with my interest in films could possibly envisage a situation in 1919 in which a national daily news-paper with a great circulation could rely on maintaining a reader interest by running a popularity ballot on British films; no more could be imagined a debate in the Parliament of the time in which an issue is made between the importation of American films and American dried eggs. In other words we emerge from the latest holocaust with at least something in our favour and to our benefit—a virile, flourish-ing new industry: British film production. The popularity ballot is good journalism because of the great public interest in our films; the debate in Parliament almost made sense because the thought was no longer absurd that we could ourselves provide our people with their film entertainment. Where do we go from here?

British films indeed are at their testing period. Their new popu-larity (or, to put it more fairly, since the popularity is deserved, their new excellence) has developed very quickly and under abnormal con-ditions. Their career between the two world wars was chequered and frustrated. There were temporary booms, but booms in the financial rather than the genuine sense—booms artificially created by an inflow of speculative capital which was never balanced by an outflow of commercially successful films—or even of films which lacked commercial success but made up for it by acquiring for the industry international prestige.

But the example of Hollywood shone like a beckoning light to would-be investors; Hollywood from being a suburb of Los Angeles became the world centre of film productions. From Britain, Russia, France, Germany, Italy—from all parts of Middle Europe—actors, actresses, writers, producers, directors migrated to this Mecca to make their fortunes. The capitalisation of Hollywood became phenomenal. The industry became one of America's most important ones, for not only did it find a great consumer market within the United States itself, but the world market increased year by year. Britain, the British Empire, all Europe were becoming Hollywood-minded and the Americans realised the significance of other export trade following the film. Publicity-minded America found her greatest national publicity campaign in her films; true, the cycle of gangster films and socially conscious classics like *The Grapes of Wrath* showed the other side of the medal, but on the whole Hollywood had found a formula by which to present America to the Americans and to the world. Hollywood became not only a centre of American wealth but also of influence. Rumour even had it that the head of one of the great film corporations had his private telephone line to the United States President of the time! Small wonder that, contemplating this phenomenon on the other side of the Atlantic, the City of London was sufficiently bemused to open her coffers to practically all comers. Why should we not be able to do what the small Californian suburb had already achieved?

Indeed it is a difficult question to answer. Creative and technical talent we did not lack; studios and equipment were a matter of bricks and mortar and engineering manufacture. There were enough cinemas in the country and filmgoing was sufficiently established a habit for large revenues to be obtained from exhibition in Britain alone. (Today several British films have each yielded *to the producers*—i.e. after deducting distribution charges—revenues of over £300,000, obtained

8

from U.K. distribution only).

But British films failed to find a world market—worse, they could not get a good representation even in our own cinemas. Over-boosted, over-costly films inexpertly made by unprofessional newcomers immobilised numbers of technicians and artists and studio space during production and earned a bad reputation for British films on their release. The question of reciprocal trading with America was as important then as it is now, but a large percentage of indifferent products gave the Americans something like a genuine excuse not to disrupt the monopoly they had built up for American products in the many thousands of American cinemas. An attempt to solve the problem by legislation gave us our first Quota Act, but the legislation was clumsy and vulnerable to abuse. The 'Quota Quickies' were the result of it, and the result of the Quota Quickies was to put British film manufacture into greater disrepute. And so the City of London dreamt of Hollywood riches by night, and by day totted up the millions she was losing in the British studios. When war broke out in 1939 we were running this industry in this precarious fashion but we were making two hundred films a year. To-day we are making some fifty odd films a year (to Hollywood's three or four hundred) and these films not only constitute the most popular entertainment in our own cinemas but are at last regarded by the Americans as a potential challenge to their supremacy in the world market. The *volte-face* has been achieved so swiftly and against the confused, neurotic and even tortured background of a nation desperately at war, that it is impossible still to bring calm judgement upon it or even to see it in proper perspective and with all its implications.

Unquestionably the appearance on the film scene of Mr. J. Arthur Rank has contributed in no small measure to the present healthy state of the film industry. Mr. Rank, before he began to interest himself in films, was already so placed in British industry that no speculative get-rich-quick approach to films, so familiar in the past, could possibly have any appeal to him. With his powerful connections in the world of finance, together with a known business hard-headedness, he could only approach his investment in films on a basis of deliberation and long-term planning. There were many of us who felt that the

9

structure was to be built on a foundation of monopoly, but Mr. Rank has disarmed his critics by undertakings given to the Government, while unashamedly expressing his belief that only by the building up of strong groups could he challenge America. It is true that to-day the position is that the Rank organisation has little rivalry, but already an attempt is being made to build up a new competitive organisation. Undoubtedly competition of this kind is the healthiest stimulant to the post-war progress of the industry, but it will be a number of years before the strong position of the Rank group can be seriously challenged, and it can therefore be assumed that in this testing period it will be these producing, distributing and exhibiting companies, united under one financial umbrella, who will largely bear the responsibility for establishing the future of our film industry.

Mr. Rank, still comparatively a newcomer to films, has speeded up his knowledge of films by an expensive education. The great sums he has poured out on production and in building up an export organisation which can cover the world may be compared to a sort of giant crammer who demands tremendous fees for getting his pupils through their exams. He has wisely divided his production interests into a series of so-called independent companies, who indeed enjoy a large measure of autonomy in production and who certainly establish keen competition amongst themselves. As for the Americans, not only are they conscious of the excellent standard of product handled by this organisation but they must also be uncomfortably aware that Mr. Rank's large theatre interests give him a strong bargaining position as far as reciprocal trade is concerned. From the day that the world war ceased the war between the film industries started in earnest.

As a film producer whose lot it has been to make British films in good times and bad for well-nigh twenty-five years, it is my belief that we could not sustain another period of depression. If the British film industry fails to gain for itself at least a fifty per cent representation on British screens (at present it is something like twenty-five per cent at least) and a firm foothold in the world market besides, it will have lost a chance which may not recur for three or four decades. The odds at present are in our favour. Such is the quality of our films to-day that we are more likely to attract talent from other countries than lose ours to Hollywood; we have at last learned to make a film which is 'national' in the best sense of that now dangerous word; we have at last gained the interest and respect of government circles who have shown their willingness to help us win our battle. It remains to be seen how quickly we can step up our production from fifty to two hundred films a year, for with all the advantages at our hand we cannot hope to achieve our goal without having quantity of manufacture as well as quality.

And this we must do bearing in mind the greatest lesson we have learned from America: at a time when our country's prestige throughout the world is our foremost consideration we must remember that the good British film, truthfully reflecting the British way of life, is the most powerful ambassador we have.

ERNEST LINDGREN

THE EARLY FEATURE FILM

1. *The Struggle for Survival*

The history of the British cinema after 1929 is the story of an uphill struggle, which cannot be understood without some knowledge of the preceding ten years or more in which that struggle began. During the First World War, America had acquired an unassailable supremacy in the world market. To say that this was entirely the result of the War is less than a half-truth; the War only accelerated the process. The Americans, with characteristic energy and an eagerness to seize new things, had developed an aptitude for the film, and especially an appreciation of the importance of movement; in D. W. Griffith they had produced a master who put American film technique far ahead of the rest of the world for many years; they had great assets in their climate and their wealth of national backgrounds; above all, for this in the long run was most important, they were developing an extensive and prosperous home market which brought in large financial returns on their own doorstep, and enabled them to compete abroad on the most advantageous terms.

When the First World War ended the British film industry, like that of other European countries, sought to re-establish itself, but found the American stranglehold too strong to break. British films were not even a financial success in the British home market. The British industry found itself, therefore, unable to build up a school of film technicians and film actors with such guarantee of employment as to become accomplished specialists at their jobs, and the British

13

films which were made fell far below American technical standards. They were by comparison slow and their staging was too obvious. In short, economic weakness was the source of technical weakness, and this in its turn was an insuperable handicap in the commercial struggle. ✳

Attempts made to break this vicious circle all ended in failure. In 1923, for example, the British National Film League was formed, and British Weeks were organised to stimulate the interest of the British film-going public in the home industry, but they proved entirely ineffective. Films continued to pour in from Hollywood to flood the market. Prices fell. Exhibitors booked ahead for longer and longer periods, which was no hardship to the Americans, who realised their main revenue at home and could afford to wait for the British receipts, but presented a serious problem to British producers not so fortunately placed. By 1925 it was estimated that 95 per cent of screen time was given over to American films. Furthermore American distributors were entrenching themselves even more firmly in an already impregnable position by the practices of mass salesmanship known as blind booking and block booking. A series of perhaps six, ten or more films would be announced, exhibitors being required to book the whole block or series when only the first one or two had been made and shown to the trade; or, again, as a condition of exhibiting a "super" film exhibitors might be obliged to accept also a certain number of much inferior films.

It was at this point, about the year 1925, that there began a movement agitating for some form of protective legislation for the British film industry; it was at last generally realised that the problem was one which must be attacked in the first instance on the purely economic level. This movement culminated in the passing of a Cinematograph Films Act in 1927, described as 'an act to restrict blind booking and advance booking of cinematograph films, and to secure the renting and exhibition of a certain proportion of British films, and for purposes connected therewith'. In the first place, it attempted to regulate trading methods between renters and exhibitors by making blind booking impossible, and by rigidly curtailing the practice of advance (or block) booking: secondly, it imposed on both renter and

14

exhibitor the obligation to acquire and show respectively, a minimum proportion, or quota, of British films in respect of the foreign films acquired and exhibited. Hence the Act became popularly known as the (First) Quota Act. The renters' quota was to rise from $7\frac{1}{2}$ per cent in 1928-29 to 20 per cent. in 1934-35; and the exhibitors' quota from 5 per cent in 1928-29 to 20 per cent in 1935-36. The Act was due to become effective as from January 1st, 1928: but even before this date, the tremors of upheaval were suddenly felt throughout the whole of the film industry. Into a world of silent shadows a voice had suddenly burst, and within a few months there was a wild scramble to wire studios and cinemas for sound, to make every film all-talking or all-singing.

The stampede towards sound gave a rude jolt to British producers preparing to settle down under the protective shade of the Quota Act, but the course of events was almost certainly, if anything, in their favour. They met the new challenge at the very outset of their new bid for recovery, and ultimately found in sound itself an ally.

In 1926, the number of British feature films was 26. In 1929 it had risen to 128, as against the minimum quota of 50 required by law. After a temporary setback in 1930, the number rose to 122 in 1931, 153 in 1932, 159 in 1933 and 190 in 1934, when exhibitors were actually screening twice the minimum amount of British films required by law. Moreover, this increase in British production came opportunely at a time when there was a decline in the supply of foreign (principally American) films caused by the economic depression and the limitations on markets imposed by the dialogue film. In 1934 the number of foreign films imported had fallen to 484, as against 550 in 1929 or 556 in 1931.

2. *The First Steps* (1929-32)

The first British sound film, Alfred Hitchcock's *Blackmail*, made a brilliant opening for the period. It firmly established the reputation of its director by demonstrating that he could, even without previous experience of sound, use the new medium with sureness and imagination, a feat the more surprising in view of the fact that *Blackmail* was planned originally as a silent film (a silent version was in fact released).

15

The best remembered sequence is that in which the heroine, who has stabbed a man in self-defence, reaches for the bread knife at breakfast the next morning, and as she touches it, suddenly jumps with terror, the state of her mind being conveyed at the same moment by distortion of the sound. Hitchcock even anticipated dubbing by substituting for the broken accent of Anny Ondra lines spoken by a young English actress. Such free treatment of the sound track at this early period was quite unusual.

In 1930 appeared Anthony Asquith's *A Cottage on Dartmoor*, but this could hardly be regarded as a sound film. Although one version was put out with sound on discs, the film was conceived as a silent film and was made essentially in the silent style. For the rest, the films of that year were not distinguished and indicate clearly the current tendency to play for an imaginative safety by filming and recording stage successes. The excessive exploitation of recorded dialogue was being practised everywhere and throwing the technique of the film back to styles of 20 years earlier. In Britain, the result was to strengthen the influence of the stage at a time when the one hope of the industry was to free itself as far as possible from that influence. The most ambitious films of the year were *The Crooked Billet* (with Carlyle Blackwell, Miles Mander and Madeleine Carroll), *Journey's End* (with Colin Clive), *On Approval* (with Tom Walls and Yvonne Arnaud), *Rookery Nook* (with Tom Walls and Ralph Lynn) and *Young Woodley* (with Frank Lawton and Madeleine Carroll), all outstanding stage successes. Even Hitchcock abandoned his more successful vein to make a film version of Seán O'Casey's *Juno and the Paycock*.

In 1931 the film version of the stage success is most conspicuously represented by *The Ghost Train* (with Jack Hulbert and Cicely Courtneidge), *The Lyons Mail* (with Sir John Martin Harvey) and *Potiphar's Wife* (with Nora Swinburne, Laurence Olivier and Norman McKinnell). Bernard Shaw, who had hitherto turned a deaf ear to importunate film producers, consented to a film version of *How He Lied to Her Husband*, directed by Cecil Lewis and with Robert Harris, Vera Lennox and Edmund Gwenn in the cast; it had all the disadvantages of the photographed play. The most successful films of the year again came from Hitchcock and Asquith. Hitchcock made a film

16

version of Galsworthy's play *The Skin Game* (with Edmund Gwenn and Phyllis Konstam), in which he managed to get away from the stage settings and to introduce scenes of English county life set against natural backgrounds; it was the first sound film to depict the English tradition, and was the forerunner of *The Good Companions*, *South Riding*, *Poison Pen* and other films of the same type.

The film of the year, however, was Anthony Asquith's *Tell England* (with Carl Harbord, Tony Bruce and Fay Compton). *Tell England*, which dealt mainly with the Gallipoli landings, was the first sincere attempt by a film director in any country to treat the First World War not as a possible subject for entertainment, but in its true proportions and perspective. Its weakness lay in its fictional story. Its strength lay in its reconstruction in an almost documentary style of the war scenes. It is worthy of note that in directing this film, Asquith had the assistance of Geoffrey Barkas, who had been a cameraman in the Great War and had directed *Battle of the Somme*. *Tell England* was not. to be equalled in its aims or achievements until the British war films of the Second World War.

1932 saw production of another Asquith picture, *Dance, Pretty Lady* (with Ann Casson and Carl Harbord), an adaptation of Compton Mackenzie's novel *Carnival*, and Alfred Hitchcock made a new thriller, *The Lodger* (with Ivor Novello and Elizabeth Allan). But the success of the year was Walter Forde's *Rome Express* (with Esther Ralston, Conrad Veidt and Gordon Harker), the first film to come from the new Gaumont-British studios at Shepherd's Bush and described at the time as 'the best full length film ever made in this country'. Apart from this there were two developments of the year which deserve mention: one was the appearance of the first of a series of films with Jack Hulbert (accompanied in this case by Cicely Courtneidge and Winifred Shotter) called *Jack's the Boy*, described by Miss Lejeune as 'the first really indigenous British screen comedy since the days of the old Betty Balfour films'; later in the same year this was followed by *Love on Wheels* (with Jack Hulbert and Gordon Harker), in a similar vein, making comedy of such familiar scenes as Selfridge's and the Green Line Coach Services. The second development was the appearance of two actuality films, *Kamet Conquered*, a

B   17

film of the attempt to climb Mount Kamet, made by F. G. Smythe, and a film of the flight by Sir Alan Cobham called *With Cobham to Khivu*.

3. *The Great Boom* (1933-36)

During these years, the British film industry had been gradually finding its feet. The number of British productions had increased considerably in quantity but not greatly in quality. In so far as there were any exceptions they came mainly from the hands of two directors —Asquith and Hitchcock. In 1933, however, one begins to find signs of a new confidence, a new sense of assuredness; one also finds at the same time evidences of a definite development of public taste. The American film was temporarily under a cloud, partly perhaps because of its failure to anticipate new audience trends, partly as a result of the economic depression. At any rate, Miss Lejeune is able to suggest in the spring of 1933 that the race for the world's markets lay between the United States and Great Britain. This may have been an over-optimistic reading of the omens but it was certainly not the sort of thing that could have been said a few years earlier.

The outstanding event of 1933 was, of course, the production of Alexander Korda's *The Private Life of Henry VIII*. I use the word 'event' advisedly, for as a film it was by no means in the first class. Its importance lay in the fact that it was the first British film to demonstrate that in spectacle and lavishness of production the British industry could legitimately hope to match the best that Hollywood could produce. It was a flag planted at the top of the hill which the industry had been climbing for five years. *The Private Life of Henry VIII* enjoyed a considerable success in America. It was the precursor of a long cycle of elaborate costume films (hitherto thought to be unpopular) on both sides of the Atlantic; and in Britain it initiated all those hopes which have been cherished since, that the British film, if only it can be sufficiently 'international' and costly, may eventually break into the foreign (and particularly American) market.

Another film of 1933 which attracted some attention on account of its original story structure was Victor Saville's *Friday the Thirteenth* (with Sonnie Hale, Jessie Matthews and Gordon Harker). A more

18

solid achievement however, was Saville's *The Good Companions* (Edmund Gwenn, Jessie Matthews and John Gielgud), an adaptation of Priestley's novel which Michael Balcon produced for Welsh-Pearson. This film was described by a contemporary critic as 'the first real example of the British picaresque on the screen', and a recent viewing shows that it still stands up well to the passage of time, which is the acid test of sincerity for any film. Victor Saville's third film of the year, *I Was a Spy*, was a popular if not impressive production, with an outstanding performance by Conrad Veidt (the other stars were Herbert Marshall and Madeleine Carroll). Veidt also appeared in Maurice Elvey's *The Wandering Jew*. Two notable actuality features of the year were a sound version of Herbert Ponting's film of the last voyage of Captain Scott, called *90° South*, and *The Tragedy of Everest*. One also notices in the year's list *Night of the Garter* and *To Brighton with Gladys*; these things should be mentioned to keep a proper sense of proportion. Tom Walls and Ralph Lynn continued their series of stage farces with *A Cuckoo in the Nest*; and Cicely Courtneidge appeared in a bright and enjoyable little piece of musical comedy, *Soldiers of the King*.

In 1934 the fashion in period spectacle was sustained by Paul Czinner's *Catherine the Great* (with Elizabeth Bergner and Douglas Fairbanks, Jnr.), Lothar Mendes' *Jew Suss* (with Conrad Veidt, Frank Vosper and Benita Hume), and Alexander Korda's *The Private Life of Don Juan* (with Douglas Fairbanks, Merle Oberon and Benita Hume); the chief merit of all these lay in their elaborate sets and costumes. With them one may group, although it was in a somewhat less lavish style, Herbert Wilcox's *Nell Gwynn* (with Anna Neagle, Cedric Hardwicke and Jeanne de Casalis). During the year there were also some notable ventures in the field of the musical, particularly Paul Stein's *Blossom Time* (with Richard Tauber and Jane Baxter), and Victor Saville's *Evergreen* (with Jessie Matthews, Sonnie Hale and Betty Balfour); and Gracie Fields starred in *Love, Life and Laughter* and *Sing as We Go*. A new young star, Nova Pilbeam, appeared in Berthold Viertel's *Little Friend*, from a script by Margaret Kennedy, and her *début* was given considerable publicity; by contrast, no publicity at all outside the Midlands was given to a modest and

19

somewhat crude effort by the Mancunian Film Corporation called *Boots, Boots,* in which a young man with a banjo made his first appearance: yet within a year or two George Formby was to be the most popular British star in Britain.

It has been left to the last to mention the one film of the year which at once took its undisputable place in film history, Robert Flaherty's *Man of Aran,* a documentary in the romantic style, marked by the sincerity and integrity which has always distinguished Flaherty's work.

In 1935 Victor Saville directed two further costume spectacles, *The Love Affair of the Dictator* (with Clive Brook and Madeleine Carroll) and *The Iron Duke* (with George Arliss, Gladys Cooper and Edmund Willard). The Korda production, *The Scarlet Pimpernel,* directed by Harold Young, was in the same style, but was distinguished by a brilliant performance by Leslie Howard in the title role.

Two more thrillers came from the hand of Alfred Hitchcock, *The Man Who Knew Too Much* (with Leslie Banks, Edna Best and Nova Pilbeam) and *The Thirty-nine Steps* (with Robert Donat, Madeleine Carroll and Godfrey Tearle), a version of John Buchan's story; in both he maintained his reputation for the skilful creation of suspense and atmosphere. Zoltan Korda's *Sanders of the River* (with Leslie Banks, Paul Robeson and Nina McKinney) was a dignified production, with some fine photography of scenery, and Robeson as actor and singer the main attraction. Elizabeth Bergner appeared in Paul Czinner's *Escape Me Never*; and Milton Rosmer directed a version of *Emil and the Detectives* which to the blank astonishment of its producers failed to achieve the success of the German original.

The music hall, whose influence has been responsible for a highly popular, though strictly national and even provincial type of film comedy, added one more figure in Will Hay, who appeared in the first of a series of comedies by Marcel Varnel, *Boys Will be Boys*. But once more it was a film with a documentary tang, Norman Walker's *Turn of the Tide* (with John Garrick and Geraldine Fitzgerald) which stole the honours of the year. Modestly produced, and taken to a large extent on location, this story of rivalry between two Yorkshire fishing families, the Fosdycks and the Lunns, was distinguished by its

20

use of natural backgrounds and its realistic portrayal of ordinary fisherfolk.

In 1936 the British sound film of the pre-war years rose to its peak in both volume and quality of achievement. The total number of British features during the year reached the unprecedented figure of 212. The most noteworthy among them are chiefly remarkable for their wide range of subject and style. Paul Czinner directed a commendable version of Shakespeare's *As You Like It* (with Elizabeth Bergner, Laurence Olivier and Sophie Stewart). A new director, Carol Reed, made *Laburnum Grove* (with Edmund Gwenn, Cedric Hardwicke and Victoria Hopper) from Priestley's play. Alexander Korda's *Rembrandt* and Robert Stevenson's *Tudor Rose* continued the costume style, but both displayed qualities other than the merely spectacular; Laughton's performance in the first, with its virtuoso recitals of long prose passages, was something of a *tour de force*, while the second treated the story of Lady Jane Grey with dignity and restraint. The same may be said also of Berthold Viertel's *Rhodes of Africa* (with Walter Huston, Oscar Homolka and Peggy Ashcroft) of which the director said, 'I tried to be faithful to the ideas of history'. This consciousness of a responsibility in the treatment of historical subjects was something new.

It was in 1936, too, that the industry discovered Mr. H. G. Wells, first in *The Man Who Could Work Miracles* (with Roland Young, Ralph Richardson and Joan Gardner) directed by Lothar Mendes; but more notably in the Korda film *Things to Come*, directed by William Cameron Menzies (with Raymond Massey, Ralph Richardson and Margaretta Scott). This film was in places slow, melodramatic, and stilted in its dialogue; against this must be set the brilliant trick and model work of Ned Mann and of the cameraman, George Perinal, and the fact that the producers had the courage to tackle a serious subject of such public importance on the screen.

A curiosity of the year was Friedrich Feher's *The Robber Symphony*, an experiment in the use of atmospheric music, which does not appear to have been shown to any wide extent after its premiere. More orthodox and more successful in the musical style were *The Song of Freedom* (with Paul Robeson) and Basil Dean's *Whom the Gods*

Love (with Victoria Hopper and John Loder) a biographical film of Mozart whose music was played by the London Philharmonic Orchestra under Sir Thomas Beecham.

Alfred Hitchcock directed two more thrillers, *Secret Agent* (with Madeleine Carroll, Peter Lorre and John Gielgud) and *Sabotage* (with Sylvia Sydney, Oscar Homolka and John Loder). In *Secret Agent*, in particular, skilful use was made of sound to contribute to atmosphere and suspense; periods of loud noise were alternated with periods of silence with great effect, and many who saw it will remember still the mournful howling of the dog when one of the characters is pushed over a cliff-top to his death.

4. *The Clouds Gather* (1937-39)

In 1937 signs of uneasiness began to appear in the industry. The British film had experienced a boom period, the number of productions had greatly increased, new British directors and stars had appeared, much talent had come from Europe, and yet in spite of all this, there was a feeling abroad that not all was well. The boom, unfortunately, had also attracted adventurers who had had no difficulty in borrowing large sums of money for ambitiously expensive productions which failed to find an adequate market. Financial speculators therefore became much more wary in their attitude towards film production of every kind. Moreover, the ultimate success of the policy of making spectacular films at high cost, which had been so actively pursued, depended on such films obtaining distribution in other countries, and above all in America. Despite the promise of *The Private Life of Henry VIII*, such distribution had not been obtained.

Doubts as to the form of further legislation also made for uncertainty. The Cinematograph Films Act of 1927 had been passed for a period of ten years only. Its success made it inevitable that similar provisions would be re-enacted, but events had proved that some modification of the old Act was essential; the only doubt was as to the form that revision would take. The chief weakness of the 1927 Act was that it had encouraged the production of 'quota quickies', bad films made quickly and cheaply for foreign renters to satisfy their quota obligations, and these productions had thrown considerable discredit on the British industry. In 1936 and 1937 producers, renters, exhibitors and employees were involved in extended discussions with the Board of Trade on these and similar problems.

In this troubled atmosphere, the industry marked time, with a slight tendency if anything, to take one step backwards; many films were simply the prescription as before: Elizabeth Bergner in Czinner's *Dreaming Lips*; Flora Robson, Laurence Olivier and Vivien Leigh in William K. Howard's *Fire Over England,* a period film with a real sense of atmosphere; Will Hay in *Good Morning Boys* and *Oh, Mr. Porter!*; Nova Pilbeam and Derrick de Marney in Hitchcock's *Young and Innocent*; Vivien Leigh and Rex Harrison in *Storm in a Teacup*, directed by Saville and Ian Dalrymple.

Besides these, however, there were a number of more novel achievements. Michael Powell suddenly came to the fore with *Edge of the World* (with Niall McGinnis, Belle Chrystal and John Laurie), a film made on the Island of Foula, with a banal story but magnificent shots of natural scenery. The first British film in Technicolor appeared, Harold Schuster's *Wings of the Morning* (with Annabella, Henry Fonda and Leslie Banks). Herbert Wilcox made *Victoria the Great* (with Anna Neagle and Anton Walbrook) an impressive piece of biographical reconstruction, which he was subsequently to follow up with *Sixty Glorious Years*. Finally, in *Farewell Again* (with Leslie Banks, Flora Robson and Patricia Hilliard), producer Erich Pommer and director Tim Whelan depicted with sympathy and understanding the reactions of several widely contrasted men in a British troopship to the news that after three years' foreign service they were to have only six hours' shore leave, and the ways in which their leave was spent. It was realistic in its approach, entirely avoiding the merely heroic, and contained a number of memorable characterisations.

On April 1st, 1938, the new Quota Act came into force. The quota system was substantially retained. For long films (over 3,000 feet) the renters' quota was to rise from 15 per cent in 1938 to 30 per cent in 1947 and the exhibitors' quota from $12\frac{1}{2}$ per cent to 25 per cent; for short films the renters' quota was to rise from 15 per cent in 1938 to 25 per cent in 1947, and exhibitors' quota from $12\frac{1}{2}$ per cent in 1938 to $22\frac{1}{2}$ per cent in 1947. The Board of Trade can take powers to alter these quotas if it should seem desirable. The outstanding feature of the Act, however, was the requirement that to qualify for quota a film must have cost at least £7,500 or £1 a foot labour costs. The aim of this provision was to eliminate the quota quickie. Producers are encouraged to go above this expenditure by provisions which enable films involving labour costs of £22,500 to £37,500 to count as double quota for renters, and films of over £37,500 labour costs to count as treble quota. Furthermore, the showing of British films abroad is encouraged by a so-called reciprocity clause which enables a foreign renter who acquires for distribution abroad a double or treble quota film for not less than £20,000, to count it once for quota; if he acquires a treble quota film for not less than £30,000, he may count it twice for quota. The following new features in the Act may also be noted:

(a) There is a separate quota for short films, which were regarded as important for the training they can provide for young directors.

(b) The new Act devotes special attention to safe-guarding the interests of film technicians and employees. The minimum cost of a quota film, it will be noted, is worked out on the basis of labour costs. A certain proportion of these labour costs must go to British subjects. A so-called Fair Wages Clause provides that producers of quota films must pay wages and provide conditions of employment not less favourable than those commonly recognised by trade union agreement or, in the absence of such agreement, such recognised wages and conditions as prevail amongst good employers.

(c) Blind and block booking continue to be made illegal.

(d) There are special provisions to allow the showing of foreign films of exceptionally small circulation without the requirement of quota.

(e) A Cinematograph Films Council, representing the general public, the industry and the workers, was set up to review progress, to advise the Board of Trade and to issue an Annual Report on the workings of the Act.

The new Act represented as satisfactory a compromise as was

24

possible between divergent points of view, and all now seemed set fair for further progress in the British industry. At the end of 1937 there were 23 studios in the country, all situated in or around London. They contained 75 production stages and a total floor area of 781,202 square feet. The three largest studios were the Amalgamated Studios at Elstree (130,000 square feet), the London Films Studios at Denham (120,000 square feet), and the Pinewood Studios at Iver Heath (72,710 square feet).

One important development of the 1938 Act was that American companies decided to engage in serious large-scale production in Britain to make films of a cost and quality which would meet the requirements of the Act. The M.G.M. Company were the first to establish a unit here, popularly known as Metro-British and to enlist the services of two of Britain's foremost producers, Victor Saville and Michael Balcon (who later became production head at Ealing Studios). The first Metro-British production was *A Yank at Oxford* (Robert Taylor, Vivien Leigh and Lionel Barrymore) directed by Jack Conway; it was followed in 1939 by King Vidor's *The Citadel* (Robert Donat, Rosalind Russell and Ralph Richardson) and Sam Wood's *Goodbye Mr. Chips* (Robert Donat, Greer Garson and Terry Kilburn). Precisely how far this making of British films by American companies with American directors and American stars might have gone (or, indeed, how far it may yet go) it is not possible to say, since the process, when still in its infancy, was to be abruptly interrupted by certain events in Europe.

Among the more genuinely native productions of merit, special mention must be made of *Bank Holiday* (with John Lodge, Margaret Lockwood and Hugh Williams). Here the director, Carol Reed, took an intelligent story (spoilt only by its melodramatic ending) and built round it a study of the English working class on holiday, which was as sound in its psychology as its pictorial detail, and full of fine touches of observation and sympathetic humour. Another rising director of talent, Robert Stevenson, made *Owd Bob*, in which Will Fyffe, hitherto known only as a music-hall comedian, gave a remarkable character study of a dour old Scottish shepherd: John Loder and Margaret Lockwood were also in the cast. A third film of British life,

25

in this case English county life, was Victor Saville's *South Riding* (with Edna Best, Ralph Richardson and Edmund Gwenn), made from a story of local politics by Winifred Holtby.

Margaret Lockwood, who was by now Britain's leading woman star, also appeared with Michael Redgrave and Paul Lukas in a Hitchcock thriller, *The Lady Vanishes*, a film which displayed once more that director's talent for subtlety in the use of both sound and visual image. Charles Laughton, with Elsa Lanchester and Robert Newton, appeared in Erich Pommer's *Vessel of Wrath*, from a story by Somerset Maugham; but it was in the characterisation, rather than in the story, that the chief merit of this film lay. *Wings of the Morning* was succeeded by two more large Technicolor productions, Tim Whelan's *The Divorce of Lady X* (with Merle Oberon, Laurence Olivier and Ralph Richardson), and Zoltan Korda's spectacle, *The Drum* (with Sabu, Raymond Massey and Valerie Hobson).

All these films, however, were a repetition or a development of previous successes. The film which was most conspicuous in 1938 for breaking new ground, was *Pygmalion*. An unknown and penniless Hungarian, Gabriel Pascal, had suddenly succeeded where so many had failed, in persuading Bernard Shaw to agree to the filming of his plays. Anthony Asquith and Leslie Howard directed jointly, and the principal actors were Leslie Howard, Wendy Hiller (whose performance immediately put her amongst our leading film stars) and Wilfred Lawson. Having regard to the numerous unknown quantities involved and the author's known predilection for a faithful reproduction of the plays as written, the result was a far better film than most had dared to expect, and its success encouraged Shaw and Pascal to proceed with further similar ventures.

It would be unjust to leave 1938 without mention of a less pretentious film which nevertheless attracted considerable attention. The story, direction and editing of David MacDonald's *This Man is News* (with Barry K. Barnes, Valerie Hobson and Alastair Sim) had a speed and slickness which had hitherto been regarded as the hall-marks of American production. On the strength of its success, the same team made *This Man in Paris* in the following year, and David MacDonald was later, as a director of the Army Film Unit, to be associated with some of the most notable feature records of the war whose clouds were already beginning to gather.

As 1939 opened, everyone hoped that war might still be averted, but the number who realised deep in their hearts how improbable this was grew month by month. Those who understood the extent of the price which had been paid at Munich knew that all excuse for complacent optimism had gone. The newspaper astrologers played on popular fear and desire by their assurances that war would not come; and school buildings and village halls were crowded by subdued gatherings assembled to be introduced to the theory of gas-warfare by newly-trained A.R.P. officials.

Such an atmosphere of apprehension was stifling to creative and experimental work in every field of peace-time activity, and the film was no exception. Anthony Asquith's *French Without Tears* (with Ray Milland, Ellen Drew and Roland Culver), a gaily-directed farce; Carol Reed's comedy, *A Girl Must Live* (with Margaret Lockwood, Renee Houston and Lilli Palmer); *Jamaica Inn* (with Charles Laughton, Leslie Banks and Maureen O'Hara) in which Hitchcock sacrificed his flair for subtlety to the interests of spectacle; Michael Powell's brilliantly directed drama of U-Boat espionage in the Orkneys, *The Spy in Black* (with Conrad Veidt, Valerie Hobson and Sebastian Shaw); Paul Stein's study of psychological perversion in an English village, *Poison Pen* (with Flora Robson, Reginald Tate and Robert Newton): these, together with the titles previously mentioned, represent the cream of the year.

On September 3rd came war, and with it a call to the British industry to face new tasks under new conditions. It had come a long way since 1929. Through the period of the initial struggles, through the boom period with its lavish productions and its rash speculations, through the two years of uncertainty which preceded the Second World War, one can trace the steady emergence, the steady upward trend of a genuinely native school of British production, acquiring skill in technique, skill in the observation of British life, new directors and new stars, and last, but not least, a school of technicians with confidence in their ability and their future (as witness the striking growth and vitality of the Association of Cine Technicians). There

27

could have been no greater test of the strength of this new school, and of its capacity for reflecting the finest elements of the national character (which is the hall-mark of a genuinely national school of film-making anywhere) than the test of war. How well it fared under the test will be told elsewhere in this book.

BLACKMAIL
B.I.P., 1929
Alfred Hitchcock

COTTAGE ON
DARTMOOR
British
Instructional
1930
Anthony Asquith

TELL ENGLAND
British
Instructional
1931
Anthony Asquith

DANCE
PRETTY LADY
B.I.P.
1931
Anthony Asquith

THE LODGER
Gainsborough
1932
Alfred Hitchcock

ROME EXPRESS
Gaumont British
1932
Walter Forde

THE PRIVATE LIFE
OF HENRY VIII
London Films
1933
Alexander Korda

MAN OF ARAN
Gaumont British
1934
Robert Flaherty

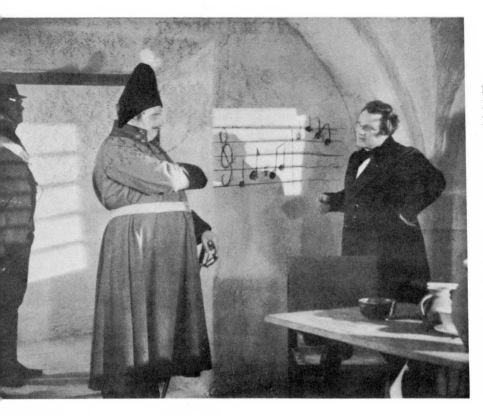

BLOSSOM TIME
B.I.P., 1934
Paul Stein

THE PRIVATE LIFE
OF DON JUAN
London Films
1934
Alexander Korda

THE THIRTY-NINE
STEPS
Gaumont British
1935
Alfred Hitchcock

THE MAN WHO
KNEW TOO MUCH
Gaumont British
1935
Alfred Hitchcock

THE SCARLET PIMPERNEL
London Films, 1935. Harold Young

c*

THINGS TO COME
London Films
1934
W. Cameron
Menzies

SECRET AGENT
Gaumont British
1935
Alfred Hitchcock

REMBRANDT
London Films
1936
Alexander Korda

FIRE OVER
ENGLAND
London Films
1937
Erich Pommer

ELEPHANT BOY
London Films
1937
Robert Flaherty
and
Zoltan Korda

FAREWELL AGAIN
Erich Pommer
1937
Tim Whelan

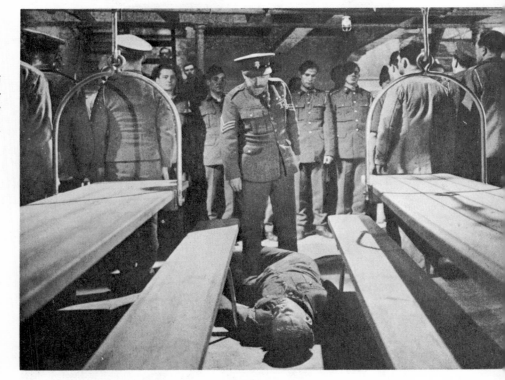

KNIGHT WITHOUT
ARMOUR
London Films
1937
Jacques Feyder

VICTORIA THE
GREAT
Imperator, 1937
Herbert Wilcox

YOUNG AND
INNOCENT
Gaumont British
1937
Alfred Hitchcock

OWD BOB
Gainsborough
1938
Robert Stevenson

VESSEL OF WRATH
Mayflower, 1938. Erich Pommer

BANK HOLIDAY
Gainsborough
1938
Carol Reed

PYGMALION
Gabriel Pascal
1938
Anthony Asquith
and
Leslie Howard

THE CITADEL
M.G.M. British
1938
King Vidor

OLD BONES
OF THE
RIVER
Gainsborough
1938
Marcel Varnel

JAMAICA INN
Pommer-Laughton
Mayflower, 1939
Alfred Hitchcock

GOODBYE
MR. CHIPS
M.G.M. British
1939
Sam Wood

FORSYTH HARDY

THE BRITISH DOCUMENTARY FILM

There is no novelty to-day in the claim that documentary is the distinctively British contribution to cinema. What began with one man and one film has become a movement with a clearly defined tradition and a considerable record of achievement. Other countries have contributed and, in its later stages, shared strongly in the development; but only in Britain has there been the continuity in aim and method which peculiarly distinguishes a deliberate movement from haphazard and sporadic effort.

It is on the British studio-feature film, also, that the documentary method has had most influence. In suggesting this, I am not forgetting, for example, the tradition of the Western in America, or the Russian films of achievement such as *Turksib* and *Men and Jobs*. I am thinking, not of categories of realist films, but of an attitude affecting the full range of production, as it has in Britain. In that sense documentary acts as a natural link between the pre-war British feature film, the period of *Man of Aran* and *Edge of the World*, *Owd Bob* and *South Riding*, and the war period, with *Nine Men* and *The Next of Kin*, *In Which We Serve* and *The Way Ahead*.

It is not difficult to find the basic reason for the continuity of documentary in Britain. In the British tradition, documentary stands essentially for a social use of film. Those who launched and have sustained the movement were interested in the film primarily as a medium of social education; although there have been periods of preoccupation with form and style, the aesthetic interest, in any final

45

analysis, has always been secondary. As the need for the social use of films has been increasingly recognised, so has the movement steadily grown.

This purposive quality distinguishes the British documentary movement from earlier uses of realist material, both in this country and abroad. Before 1929 there were, for example, Flaherty's pictures of the Eskimos and the Samoans, stories of real people told from the inside. There were the impressionistic renderings of city life, Caval-canti's *Rien que les Heures* and Ruttmann's *Berlin*. In Britain there was the fine work done in the *Secrets of Nature* series by Bruce Woolfe and his collaborators; and Andrew Buchanan's enterprising screen journalism in the *Cinemagazines*. Since it was not their object, it is no criticism of these films to suggest that they were innocent of the social purpose which was to become characteristic of the documentaries.

I referred above to a beginning with one man and one film: you cannot go very far in documentary without taking account of John Grierson, founder of the movement in Britain and, since 1929, its chief source of inspiration. Grierson himself would prefer that priority were given to Sir Stephen Tallents, whose courage and vision meant so much to the movement in its first years. It was, in any case, a for-tunate meeting at the Empire Marketing Board early in 1927, when Tallents, enlisting media of popular interpretation to help him in his task of 'bringing the Empire alive', found in Grierson a man with the imagination and zeal to develop film for this end.

It is difficult to appreciate to-day just how revolutionary a film *Drifters* appeared when it was shown at the end of 1929. It reached the cinemas simultaneously with the first of the British sound films, those daring photographic records of Co-optimists' shows and Ald-wych farces. In such surroundings Grierson's story of the North Sea herring fishermen seemed to belong to another world—as indeed it did. This was workaday Britain on the screen. The feeling of contact with real life, now a commonplace of cinema-going, then had the sharp impact of novelty.

In technique as much as in content, *Drifters* also struck a new note in British cinema. Grierson's study of national schools of cinema had brought him closely into touch with the work of the Russian directors.

46

His own film showed the influence of the principles of symphonic structure and dynamic editing evolved by Eisenstein and Pudovkin. Here is the beginning of that characteristic duality in documentary, that combination of social purpose and aesthetic experiment, which has persisted throughout its development.

In the long run, more important than either content or form was the sponsorship of the film. If we except the war record pictures, *Drifters* marked the beginning of Government use of the film medium in Britain. However unremarkable Government sponsorship appears to-day, when officially produced films are counted in hundreds each year, the production of *Drifters* under Government auspices in 1929 was something revolutionary. It is sometimes forgotten that behind the impressive achievement of the documentary film movement over the past sixteen years lies the unwavering support of the British Government.

The success of *Drifters* convinced Grierson that he had found in the film the medium most suited to his sociological purpose. 'I liked the idea of a simple dramatic art based on authentic information,' he has written. 'I liked the idea of an art where the dramatic factor depended exactly on the depth with which information was interpreted. I liked the notion that, in making films of man in his modern environment, one would be articulating the corporate character of that environment and finding again, after a long period of sloppy romanticism and the person in private, an aesthetic of the person in public.'

After *Drifters* there was a period of slow growth, while one man became a unit and an idea began to expand into a movement. Grierson gathered about him a group of young men who shared his outlook and were gradually trained in his methods: Basil Wright, Arthur Elton, Stuart Legg, Paul Rotha, Harry Watt, Donald Taylor, Edgar Anstey, John Taylor, and others. It was a period of hard work and intense application; of long hours and low wages. But the foundations of the documentary movement were firmly laid during those early years of exacting apprenticeship. While Grierson's energies were absorbed in training and in the creative work of production, Tallents protected the continuity of the effort and gave it a chance to expand.

When, at the end of this period, the new films began to appear, it was possible to see the movement taking shape. In the task of bringing the Empire alive, a beginning was made with Britain. *O'er Hill and Dale* (1931-32), Basil Wright's account of a day in the life of a Scots shepherd, was a notable study of a man shown in relation to his environment. It fulfilled Grierson's requirement that a documentary must do more than describe: it must reveal. In *Industrial Britain* (1933), on which Robert Flaherty worked before leaving for the Aran Islands, the traditional skills of the potter and the glass-blower were matched with the similar sense of craftsmanship to be found in the making of modern aeroplane engines. *Shadow on the Mountain* (1931), Elton's report on Professor Stapledon's pasture experiments at Aberystwyth, was concerned to interpret the results of research to those who might profit from them: another tradition which, originating in the E.M.B. purpose, has persisted in documentary.

Before the Empire Marketing Board was dissolved in July 1933, Grierson's unit had produced nearly a hundred films. Some, like Basil Wright's *Lumber* (1931), were re-edited versions of material obtained from Canada. Others, like the same director's *Windmill in Barbadoes* (1933), *Cargo from Jamaica* (1933) and the other films of the West Indies, were a first contribution towards the interpretation of the Empire overseas. It was true of all the films of this period that they were experimental and exploratory. Experimental also was the setting up of the Empire Film Library at the Imperial Institute—the first move in the development of a widespread distribution of documentary films outside the ordinary cinemas.

Although this first phase was short—less than four years—it was long enough to establish documentary as a movement. Something like a dozen directors had been trained and were able to undertake work independent of the main unit (Stuart Legg's *The New Generation* (1932) for the Chesterfield Education Authority, Elton's *The Voice of the World* (1932) for the Gramophone Company, and Rotha's *Contact* (1932-33) for Imperial Airways were early examples). The development was full of promise. Among those who appreciated its value and significance, there was acute concern lest the Grierson unit should not continue as a training school and as a clearing-house for documentary theory and practice on the demise of the E.M.B.

These fears were set at rest when the unit was invited to go with Sir Stephen Tallents to the Post Office, or, as Grierson has it, 'Tallents insisted on it'. To many sympathetic observers it seemed doubtful if the Post Office could offer documentary sufficient scope for expansion. Grierson himself found his new surroundings at first 'singularly unpromising'. But the challenge was taken up with characteristic vigour and vision. 'We gradually began to see, behind the infernal penny-in-the-slot detail in which the Post Office is so symbolic of our metropolitan civilisation, something of the magic of modern communications. We saw the gale warning behind the Central Telegraph Office, the paradox of nationalism and internationalism behind the cable service, the choral beauty of the night mail, and the drama tucked away in the files of the ship-to-shore radio service. Most significant of all, Cavalcanti achieved the singular feat of getting under the skin of the Accountant General's department and bringing the routine clerk in most human terms to the screen.'

Vision of this kind was to characterise the story of national and international communications as told by the G.P.O. Film Unit during the next six years. Among the most memorable films of this period were Legg's *Cable Ship* (1933) which caught the drama of the submarine cable link with the Continent; Evelyn Spice's *Weather Forecast* (1934), the exciting story behind the gale warning; Anstey's *Six-Thirty Collection* (1934), an imaginative record of the treatment of a single evening's mail in London; *B.B.C.— The Voice of Britain* (1934-35), on the social implications underlying radio in Britain; *Night Mail* (1936), the Harry Watt-Basil Wright story of the overnight journey of the travelling post office from London to Scotland; and Harry Watt's *North Sea* (1938) on the ship-to-shore radio service.

During this period there was constant experiment with new techniques. In the E.M.B. films experiment was largely confined to the visuals and the influence of the silent film was strong. Even within this limit, however, certain styles could be noted: lyrical in Wright's work, for example, and analytical in Elton's. It is interesting in this connection to recall a comment of Grierson's written when *Industrial Britain* was first shown late in 1933: 'With *Industrial Britain* those of us engaged in documentary work have more or less finally freed ourselves from the tyranny of the impressionist method. We look now, not for symphonic effects, but for themes; expecting larger results from a simple painstaking observation of processes, and a laborious building of their issue and their importance, than from an orchestration of their more superficial good looks.' The change of emphasis was significant, although *Industrial Britain* was by no means the last film to use the impressionist method.

When the G.P.O. Film Unit obtained a studio and recording equipment, experiment with sound as well as with picture became possible. One of the first films to demonstrate an imaginative use of sound far in advance of contemporary practice in the studios was Wright's *Song of Ceylon* (1934-35). Here the sound-track was not used merely to provide the visuals with the obvious accompaniment in dialogue and music but made an individual and different contribution to the expression of the theme—the influence of Western civilisation on native life. This imaginative use of sound was continued notably in *Pett and Pott* (1934), *Coalface* (1935), and *Night Mail*. Much stimulus was given to this work by Cavalcanti, who joined the unit from France and lent his skill and craftsmanship to many productions, from *Pett and Pott* to *The First Days*. Others who lent their special talents to the experimental work in progress included W. H. Auden, Walter Leigh, and Benjamin Britten. Len Lye made several abstract colour films, of which *Rainbow Dance* (1936) in particular was outstanding.

Some of the films produced during the middle 'thirties strike us to-day as self-consciously mannered and pretentious. Perhaps limitations imposed by the subject-matter had the effect of swinging the unit further into aestheticism than would have occurred had the range of themes been broader and more exacting. It must be recognised, however, that, outside of Disney, the work of the G.P.O. Film Unit during this period represents an imaginative use of sound unequalled in cinema at any other time or place. In particular, *Night Mail* with its ingenious choral effects, finely arranged visuals, and evocative music, will remain an outstanding example of the imaginative use of sound and picture.

As a movement, documentary was expanding rapidly in the middle 'thirties. Grierson at the G.P.O. was still the chief source of inspiration and leadership; but many of the directors were finding opportunities to develop the documentary idea under other sponsorships. Imperial Airways and the Orient Line were early in the field, to be followed, among other industries and organisations, by Shell-Mex, Anglo-Iranian, the British Commercial Gas Association, the Films of Scotland Committee, the Canadian Government, the Ministry of Labour, the Travel and Industrial Development Association, the National Book Council, and the Colonial Empire Marketing Board. What was remarkable in this development was that, to use Grierson's words, 'whatever the sponsorship, these documentary film people have, in nearly every case, sought to find some public importance in their observations'. Here, if anywhere, was proof that documentary was a movement and not an effort susceptible to the changing winds of sponsorship.

Consider, for example, the cases of *Housing Problems* and *Enough to Eat*. To-day we would expect to see films on slum clearance and nutritional problems appear under the imprint of the Ministries of Health and Food, and credit for their initiation would go to far-sighted administrations. In 1935-36, these films were made for the Gas Association and credit for their social truth must go to the directors who made them. By producing these and similar films of social reconstruction, the documentary movement grew in responsibility and influence. No one seeing *Housing Problems* and *Enough to Eat* could doubt the intensity of feeling behind their production. In their search for emphasis, the team which made the housing film (Elton, Anstey, Ruby Grierson, and John Taylor) developed the technique of direct interview which, in its forceful statement, was poles apart from the impressionism of the early films.

The same consciousness of social purpose could be found in almost every film produced under similar auspices during this period: in Rotha's *Shipyard* (1934-35), an account of the sociological and economic effects of the building of a liner on the community, made for the Orient Line; in Alexander Shaw's *The Future's in the Air* (1936-37), a forward-looking picture of civil aviation, made for Imperial Airways; in Wright's *Children at School* (1937), which, made for the Gas Association, surveyed schools and schooling in England

D.

51

and focused attention on out-of-date building; in Ruby Grierson's *To-day We Live* (1937), a new conception of community life in country village and mining town, made for the National Council of Social Service; in *The Londoners* (1938), John Taylor's stimulating picture of the London County Council's activities, past and present, made for the Gas Association; and in Stanley Hawes's *Speed the Plough* (1939), an account of the mechanisation of farming in Britain, made for the Petroleum Films Bureau.

As Grierson has pointed out, this could not have happened 'without a sense of the deeper levels of communication' on the part of the public relations departments serving these organisations. Without such enlightened co-operation, documentary could not have made the progress it did during the 'thirties.

As a result of this many-sided development, the need for a central co-ordinating and advisory body became obvious. To meet this need, Grierson resigned from the G.P.O. Film Unit in June 1937, and founded Film Centre. His aim was to provide a consultative and policy-forming centre which would undertake investigation and research, offer advice on the use of documentary film, and supervise but not directly engage in production. These have continued to be the functions of Film Centre, where, during Grierson's absence in Canada, Wright, Elton, and Anstey have, at different periods, been in control.

As an example of the work done at Film Centre, I might refer to the film programme undertaken for the Films of Scotland Committee. Set up during the year of the Glasgow Empire Exhibition by the Scottish Development Council in consultation with the Secretary of State for Scotland, the Committee had as its aim the projection of Scotland in terms of film. The seven films which resulted brought to the screen a record of a country at once concise and comprehensive. *The Face of Scotland* (1938), directed by Basil Wright, was an exciting interpretation of the national character and traditions. Donald Alexander's *Wealth of a Nation* (1938) surveyed the effects of Scotland's coal rush and collated contemporary effort for the economic replanning of the country. Mary Field's *They Made the Land* (1938) told the story of Scotland's agriculture in terms both of tradition and

52

modern research. *The Children's Story* (1938), directed by Alexander Shaw, described what was being done in the schools to maintain one of the finest traditions in Scottish life. *Sea Food* told the story of fishery research, and the series was completed with a film on the Scottish countryside and another on sport in Scotland. Contrasted in style and treatment, the films achieved through the single production control a finely co-ordinated and challenging picture of a nation's life.

There were other distinctive groups of films in the steadily growing volume of documentary production. Working for a period with G.-B. Instructional, Paul Rotha made *Rising Tide* (1933-34), which used dock extensions at Southampton as a basis for comment on the interdependence of Empire trade, and *The Face of Britain* (1934-35), which discussed the planning of British resources with particular reference to the respective power of coal and electricity. Strand Films, first of the independent documentary units, made a series of delightful films at the Whipsnade Zoo, produced by Stuart Legg and directed by Evelyn Spice and Ruby Grierson. The latter's *The Zoo and You* (1938) remains in the memory for its sprightly satirical approach. There was distinction of a different kind in the scientific films produced by Arthur Elton. His early films, including *Upstream* (1931) and *Aero Engine* (1933-34) had a notable lucidity and concern for the ordered statement of fact. These qualities were to be found also in, for example, *Transfer of Power* and *Springs*, produced in 1938-39 by the Shell Marketing Film Unit. Marion Grierson made an attractive group of films for the Travel Association. These included refreshing descriptions of London life, such as *So This is London* (1933-34) and *For All Eternity* (1934), a moving impression of the cathedrals of England.

I have referred earlier to the work of Bruce Woolfe and his collaborators. Although this included a number of documentaries—*The Mine* (1936) by J. B. Holmes, for example, and Mary Field's *This Was England* (1935) and other films of farming life and problems—the G.-B. Instructional effort is identified mainly with the *Secrets of Nature* and *Secrets of Life* series. Launched in 1919, the series, under different titles, has continued in uninterrupted production. Edgar Chance, H. A. Gilbert, Walter Higham, and Oliver Pike contributed

53

by their painstaking efforts a notable group of bird films. Percy Smith's films enabled us to watch, for example, a nasturtium grow from seed to flower in five minutes, and the amazing peregrinations of black mould on plum jam. Some of the movements caught by his microscopical camera—a suddenly blossoming flower, the sensitive probing of a root tip, the beating heart of a newt embryo—are among the imperishable memories of film-going during this period.

Meanwhile, within the G.P.O. Film Unit, a significant development in documentary was taking place. Hitherto, in the majority of documentaries, the theme had been expressed through pictorial or spoken fact, not by a story involving personal relationships. *The Saving of Bill Blewitt* (1937) was the first G.P.O. film to make successful use of real people as characters in a story. *North Sea*, which Harry Watt made in the following year, consolidated the experiment of the earlier and slighter film. The story of the North Sea trawlers and the ship-to-shore radio service, their life-line in time of danger, was told in terms of people and personal relationships. Here were people both typical and real—not only in the conflict at sea, which is part of the trawlerman's daily round, but also in the relationships of life at home. *North Sea* was to have a considerable influence on all subsequent documentary development. It had demonstrated that the use of a story and actors was not incompatible with the documentary idea. The way was prepared for *Men of the Lightship*, *Target for To-night* and *Western Approaches*.

When the war began documentary had passed beyond the experimental stage. There was a solid body of achievement to justify Grierson's belief in the documentary idea. Some 300 films had been produced, portraying the life and purposes of Britain with truth and imagination. The battle for authenticity had not been won without at least a skirmish or two. The most notable was the controversy on the subject of what British films should be sent for exhibition at the New York World's Fair in 1939. The issue was summed up in Grierson's phrase: Knee breeches or working clothes—in other words, the tradition and pageantry of the British Council films, or the story of Britain's social aims and achievements as told in the documentaries. Public opinion in the United States did secure exhibition for the social documentaries; and there were other evidences of international recognition of the worth of the British documentary movement.

At first there seemed no doubt about the role documentary was to play during the war. The G.P.O. Film Unit, with Cavalcanti as producer, made *The First Days*, brilliantly interpreting the atmosphere of London during September 1939. Filming freely in the streets and parks, cameramen registered the calm determination of the Londoners, the feeling of friendliness, the sense of unity in a common cause. Omitting Korda's curious compilation, *The Lion Has Wings* (which Vincent Sheehan reports having seen run as a comedy—in Berlin!), the next film to appear was *Squadron* 992 (1940), Harry Watt's dramatic reconstruction of the Firth of Forth raid in the early weeks of the war and the defensive role of the balloon barrage. It was a brilliantly arranged and exciting film, with a warm human quality we were beginning to think as characteristic of Watt's work. In the final analysis it was a defensive film, like *Britain Can Take It* (1940), and others similar in theme to follow; but, as a dramatic episode, it would have taken its place naturally in a film programme where the compensating aggressive notes were struck elsewhere—if there had been such a programme.

It was many months after the outbreak of war before the Ministry of Information suggested that it had evolved a policy which would make adequate use of the documentary movement. The leaders of the movement themselves were in no doubt that a magnificent opportunity was being frittered away. In issue after issue, *Documentary News Letter* underlined its criticism of lost opportunities. Perhaps it was difficult for the Government, when the future of the country hung rather delicately in the balance, to devote much attention to a policy for documentary. Perhaps their very eagerness made the documentary producers protest over much. Whatever the reasons, and their justification, it is true that documentary began only gradually and fitfully to make its contribution to the war effort.

That the documentary producers did protest is proof of the seriousness of their sociological purpose. Consider, for example, the following quotation from *Documentary News Letter* for July 1940:

'It may be argued that it is now too late to inaugurate a plan of long-term democratic propaganda, that our public information and propaganda services must now devote all their energies to the immediate needs of a desperate national fight for life. Yet a nation fighting desperately to defend the present, lacks the inspiration which springs from a vision of the future. Now, more than ever, it is necessary to repair past errors and fortify national morale with an articulation of democratic citizenship as a constructive force which can mould the future.' These are brave words, and reflect nothing but credit on the movement.

With Jack Beddington in charge of the Films Division at the Ministry of Information, progress began to be recorded, although there was as yet no evidence of consideration of long-term issues. A series of five-minute weekly film messages, to be shown in cinemas all over the country, was announced, and a good beginning was made with J. B. Priestley's *Britain at Bay*. Before these films were replaced by monthly issues of fifteen minutes in length, over eighty were produced. They varied widely in subject-matter and in quality. There were Government appeals: *Salvage With a Smile*, *Mr. Proudfoot Shows a Light*, and *The Nose Has It* (Arthur Askey cleverly adapting Benchley's lecture technique). There were films of Britain on the defensive: *Dover Front Line*, *Words for Battle*, and *The Heart of Britain*. There were recruiting films: *A.T.S.*, *Hospital Nurse*, and *Land Girl*. There were reports from the war fronts, notably Harry Watt's *Lofoten*. And there were films reflecting the Allied war effort: *Diary of a Polish Airman* and *The Five Men of Velish*.

In addition to these short films, which were the main documentary activity for over two years, there were a number of more ambitious productions made by the G.P.O., or the Crown Film Unit, as it was now known. The first of these was *Men of the Lightship* (1940), produced by Cavalcanti before he went to Ealing Studios and directed by David Macdonald. Its story of a Nazi attack on an unarmed lightship was still the 'Britain Can Take It' theme; but it succeeded significantly in stimulating a feeling of active protest. This was followed by another story of the sea, *Merchant Seamen* (1941), whose theme was the hazards of the Merchant Service and its ability to hit back. The story was told through the experiences and personalities of a group of seamen who are torpedoed but escape to serve again. Directed by J. B. Holmes, this was a mature and effective film, notable technically for the handling of the players. It was followed in a month or two by Harry Watt's *Target for To-night* (1941), which remains the best-known documentary made during the war or before it. This account of a raid over Germany came at the right psychological moment, when we were wearying of the 'Britain Can Take It' idea and longing to hear of aggressive action. Watt's film caught the drama of what was then a large-scale raid and the dry phrases of the official *communiqués* came alive.

The success of *Target for To-night* both with audiences in this country and abroad had a sharply stimulating effect. The graph of film production at the M. of I. rose steadily. Many of the films had purely utilitarian purposes: films on how to dig and how to deal with a fire bomb, how to get more eggs from your hens and how to enjoy a Woolton pie, how to keep rabbits for extra meat and how to get orange juice for the children. The documentary units, now growing fast in numbers, lent their skill, often with ingenious result, to the making of these films of advice or exhortation. They were shown for the most part on the non-theatrical circuit built up by the Ministry's 150 travelling film units.

In addition to these instructional films, there were others in the style and on the scale of *Merchant Seamen* and *Target for To-night*, dealing with campaigns or Service achievements. *Ferry Pilot* (1942), directed by Pat Jackson, told the story of a service vitally important in the early war years. *Wavell's 30,000* (1942), first of the campaign films, described Wavell's advance into Libya. *We Sail at Midnight* (1942), directed by Julian Spiro, told the story of the operation of the Lease-Lend arrangement in terms of the supply of essential tools to a British tank factory. J. B. Holmes's *Coastal Command* (1942) described the patient and tireless work of the R.A.F.'s coastal patrols. In this film in particular, the understatement characteristic of documentary was carried to such an extreme that the story failed to come alive on the screen: it described but failed to reveal. Its chief virtue was its magnificent aerial photography. *Operational Heights*

(1943) supplemented *Squadron 992* by telling the story of one of the balloon ships guarding vital stretches of the sea approaches. *Close Quarters* (1943) suffered from the disadvantage of reaching the cinemas two months after the studio-produced story of submarine patrol work, *We Dive at Dawn*, but otherwise demonstrated the greater power inherent in the imaginative use of real material.

Malta G.C. (1943), a tribute to the island's heroic role in the battle of the Mediterranean, was an appropriate forerunner of the series of combat films. The standard was at once set high by *Desert Victory* (1943), which told with simple lucidity and sober pride the story of the advance from El Alamein. The film rested firmly on the basis of the material shot by the combat cameramen: legitimate additions were the animated diagrams explaining the tactical aspects and a staged sequence depicting the Eighth Army's night attack. *Tunisian Victory* (1944), a joint British-American production, enjoyed the advantage of a campaign which offered a perfect scenario, and made the most of it, despite the interpolated nostalgic sequences. With *Left of the Line* (1944) the battle scene moved to Europe and the story of the British and Canadian drive from the Normandy beaches to Brussels was told with restraint. *The True Glory* (1945), most ambitious of the series of war films, also adopted the most ambitious shape. It told the story of the invasion of Europe and the victorious campaign in the West in the terms of the men who fought and won the battles. Directed by Carol Reed and Garson Kanin, the film sustained a fine balance and only the passages of declamatory commentary earned criticism. Finally, *Burma Victory* (1945), by David Macdonald and Roy Boulting, succeeded both in making clear the confused phases of the Burma campaign between 1942 and the end of the Japanese war, and in being a good film, intelligently constructed and vivid and compact in its narrative.

An important addition to these war films was *Western Approaches* (1944), the Crown Film Unit's most ambitious production and its only picture in Technicolor. Written and directed by Pat Jackson, its aim was to bring alive the drama of our struggle against the U-boats. The strength of its story of a torpedoed crew, rescue from a convoy, and the destruction of a submarine lay in its authenticity. Here was a magnificent justification of the documentary method.

Drama on the home front was not neglected. Several of the films were made by Humphrey Jennings, the unrepentant impressionist of the Crown Film Unit. Experiments in *Spare Time* (1939) and *Listen to Britain* (1942) were followed by the more ambitious *Fires Were Started* (1943), which told the story of the blitz by focusing our attention on a single incident. By making us familiar with the routine of the station and the individual firemen, he added to the suspense and excitement of the action during the raid. Jennings's developing skill and versatility as a director were further demonstrated in *The Silent Village* (1943), a memorial to the people of Lidice, played out against the sympathetic background of a South Wales mining village; and in *The True Story of Lili Marlene* (1944), in which much technical skill and ingenuity were squandered on trying to find some significance in the popularity of a Nazi song. *A Diary for Timothy* (1945) attempted a survey of the last six months of the war and despite the controlling influence of Basil Wright as producer, Jennings's flair for impressionism again diverted him from the exacting demands of his theme.

With war demands pressing increasingly, there was little opportunity to continue the social documentaries of the immediate pre-war period. *The Harvest Shall Come* (1942), directed by Max Anderson, told the story of the decay of British agriculture over the past forty years and posed the problem of farm labour when the policy of importing the bulk of the nation's food was resumed. Like *North Sea*, it was a genuine story film made with a documentary purpose. *Children of the City* (1944) discussed the reasons for the war-time growth of child crime and the constructive measures taken in Scotland to deal with the problem. In *Tyneside Story* (1944), Gilbert Gunn examined sympathetically the post-war outlook for shipbuilding and the shipyard worker. Ralph Keene's *Proud City* (1945) took as its theme the opportunity war has presented for rebuilding London. More important than any of these films, however, were Paul Rotha's two productions, *World of Plenty* (1943) and *Land of Promise* (1945). The first dealt with food—pre-war distribution and consumption, the effects of war, and the possibilities of control and fair distribution after the war. It was a masterly piece of exposition, a milestone in the development of

59

the factual film. *Land of Promise* dealt similarly with the problem of houses and homes, proceeding as in the food film by question, argument, and the calling of evidence.

If, at the outbreak of war, the documentary movement was under-employed, by the end of 1945 too many films were being made and standards suffered accordingly. Only the exceptional productions could compare with the best work done in the immediate pre-war years. There were two main reasons for this decline in quality. One was the restraint inevitable under Government sponsorship. To see a film through the protracted processes of investigation and production, with endless reference back, called for toughness and integrity rarely found in adequate combination. The other reason was the tiredness of directors, who had no time and little inclination to bend imagination to the work in progress and make their films reveal as well as describe. Too many documentaries in the later war period were little more than pictures held together by commentary.

Despite this tendency, noted with regret both inside and outside the movement and possibly inevitable in the conditions prevailing, documentary emerged from the war with a greatly enhanced reputation. Documentary had become familiar to audiences in every part of the country, from London's West End to isolated village audiences in the Shetlands. If documentary did not play the part which the most enthusiastic members of the movement hoped it would during the war, it was not because of their lack of enthusiasm but because of restricted opportunity. Let me close this survey with an apt comment of Grierson's, made following a visit to this country towards the end of the war: 'It has been a wonderful thing to see, in spite of the war and the special difficulties of film making in Britain, the documentary people there have remembered the essentials of social reference. They have not been fooled into the fallacy that fighting films give anything more than one layer of the present reality. But I keep on feeling that the documentary group as a whole is not at the centre where political and social planning is being thought out and legislated, or not close enough to the centre. It is not good enough to be on the outside looking in, waiting on someone else's pleasure for an opportunity to serve social progress.'

60

DRIFTERS
E.M.B. Film Unit
1929
John Grierson

NORTH SEA
G.P.O. Film Unit
1938
Harry Watt

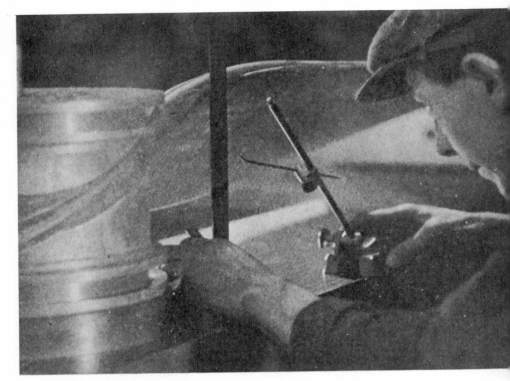

AERO ENGINE
E.M.B. Film Unit
1933-34
Arthur Elton

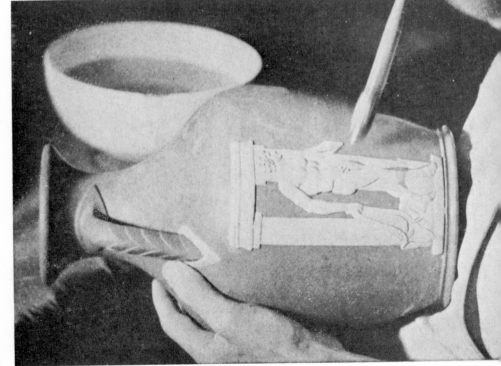

INDUSTRIAL
BRITAIN
E.M.B. Film Unit
1933
Robert Flaherty
and John Grierson

WINDMILL IN
BARBADOES
E.M.B. Film Unit
1933
Basil Wright

SONG OF CEYLON
Ceylon Tea
Propaganda Board
1934-35
Basil Wright

THE FACE OF
BRITAIN
G.-B. Instructional
1934-35
Paul Rotha

SHIPYARD
G.-B. Instructional
1934-35
Paul Rotha

B.B.C. : THE VOICE
OF BRITAIN
G.P.O. Film Unit
1934-35
Stuart Legg

COAL FACE
Empo, 1936
Alberto Cavalcanti

NIGHT MAIL
G.P.O. Film Unit
1936
Harry Watt
and Basil Wright

THEY MADE THE
LAND
G.-B. Instructional
1938
Mary Field

WE LIVE IN TWO
WORLDS
G.P.O. Film Unit
1937
Alberto Cavalcanti

THE SAVING OF
BILL BLEWITT
G.P.O. Film Unit
1937
Harry Watt

ENOUGH TO EAT
Gas, Light & Coke
Co., 1936
Edgar Anstey

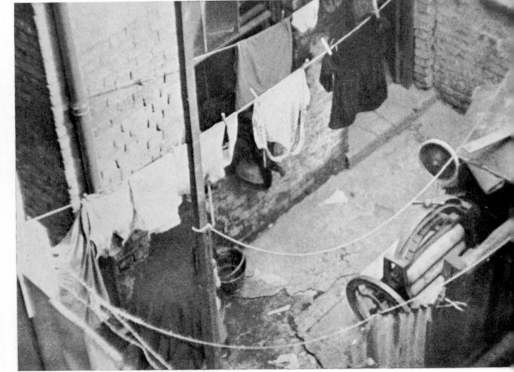

HOUSING
PROBLEMS
British
Commercial
Gas Association
1935
Edgar Anstey
Arthur Elton
and John Taylor

SECRETS OF LIFE
G.-B. Instructional
Head of
a Water Flea

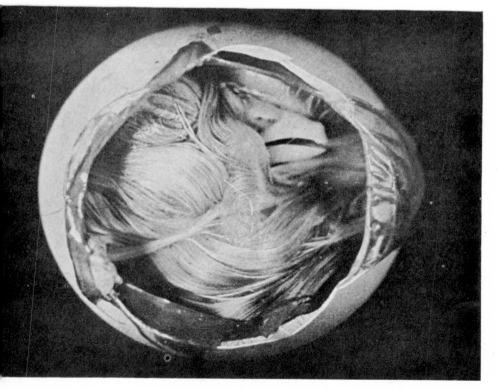

SECRETS OF LIFE
G.-B. Instructional
Development of a
Chick

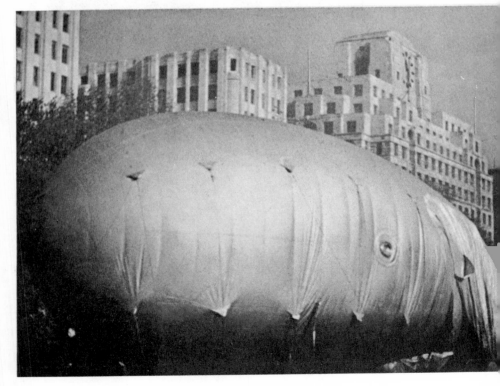

TARGET FOR
TO-NIGHT
Crown Film Unit
1941
Harry Watt

THE FIRST DAYS
G.P.O. Film Unit
1939-40

WESTERN
APPROACHES
Crown Film Unit
1944
Pat Jackson

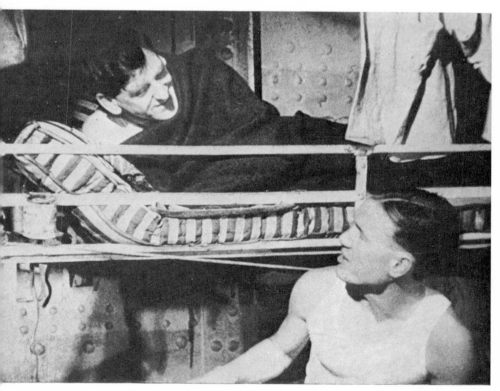

MERCHANT
SEAMEN
Crown Film Unit
1941
Jack Holmes

FERRY PILOT
Crown Film Unit
1942
Pat Jackson

NIGHT FLIGHT
R.A.F. Film Unit
1944

BEFORE THE RAID
Crown Film Unit
1943
Jiri Weiss

TUNISIAN VICTORY
British and
American
Service Film Units
1944

FIRES WERE
STARTED
Crown Film Unit
1943
Humphrey
Jennings

THE SILENT
VILLAGE
Crown Film Unit
1943
Humphrey
Jennings

GREEK
TESTAMENT
Ealing Studios
1943
Alberto Cavalcanti

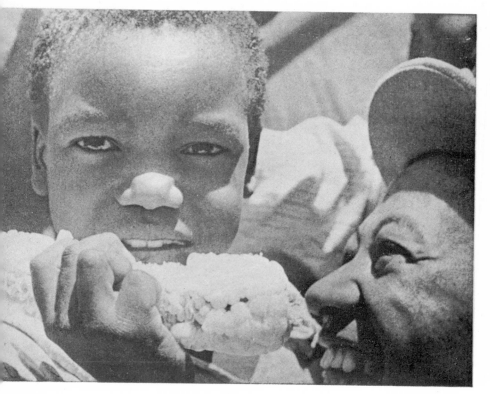

SOUTH AFRICA
Crown Film Unit
1943

LAND GIRL
Paul Rotha
Productions
1941
John Page

POWER FOR THE
HIGHLANDS
Paul Rotha
Productions
1944
Jack Chambers

OUT OF CHAOS
Two Cities Films
1944
Jill Craigie

A TYNESIDE
STORY
Spectator Films
1944
Gilbert Gunn

OUR COUNTRY
Strand Films
1945
John Eldridge
and
Donald Taylor

CROFTERS
Green Park
Productions
1944
Ralph Keene

BIRTHDAY
Data Films
1945
Budge Cooper

CHILDREN OF
THE CITY
Paul Rotha
Productions
1944
Budge Cooper

LAND OF PROMISE
Films of Fact
1945
Paul Rotha

LAND OF PROMISE
Films of Fact
1945
Paul Rotha

ROGER MANVELL

THE BRITISH FEATURE FILM FROM 1940 TO 1945

Introduction

The War started with closed cinemas and shaded lights, with people quiet and serious in the expectation of a new and unknown violence. When the violence did not come during the first weeks, the cinemas were soon re-opened and people learned that their need for entertainment exceeded their dislike of the black streets and the unlit pavements. Later it even exceeded their fear of the bombs themselves, for the cinemas continued to show their films after the warning of approaching aircraft, and few people left their seats for the safety of air-raid shelters. The cinema was an ingrown part of our national life, and the weekly attendance rose during the war years to some thirty million. Almost half the population from early youth to old age went at least once a week to the pictures. They went, it was said, to escape from the pressing responsibilities of being alive in war-time Britain. They went because they were tired. They went, it was said, for a hundred reasons except the true one, which was that a regimented life, in or out of the Services, was a dull life, an unemotional life, and within the dark walls of the cinemas stories of human beings were shown with such emotional emphasis that this life seemed once more valuable and precious. For most people the War meant hard work undertaken in the emotional vacuum of a broken home or strange surroundings. The arts generally flourished under the patronage of a larger public than had ever been known before in Britain. They flourished because they gave emotional nourishment to people who had to pack natural living into seven days' leave, and marry their lovers on the eve of long departures.

The cinema, like all the arts, can offer emotional escape or fulfilment. It can seduce the heart by presenting characters and situations according to the routine patterns of showmanship. Or it can reveal the unexpected beauty of human character and emphasise the fundamental problems and values of human relationships. The new serious public of Britain did not forsake their old enjoyment of the entertainment patterns devised by film-makers in a peaceful Hollywood, but they were prepared also to play their part in creating a new British cinema born out of the ashes of the old. Because they had themselves to acquire a certain emotional maturity to bear the deprivations and self-adjustments of war-time, they made the new and more mature British cinema successful by their support at the box-office at a time when production costs were rising and making a wide and popular patronage essential.

The renaissance of British films was not an accident. It was the deliberate design of good producers and good artists who understood by intelligence and intuition what the quality of the new Britain was. They made it their business to reveal on the screen this new spirit in the British people. They faced great difficulties in order to do so, but the difficulties were themselves part of the endeavour they were epitomising in their films. The various themes arising out of the war owed much to the spirit of the documentary movement which had for ten years been studying the British character and the British scene for film purposes. From the best of these documentaries the qualities of understatement, of pride revealed by implication rather than by display, were taken over into the story film. It was in these documentary-feature war films that the renaissance of our cinema first took permanent form.

The studios faced great difficulties. Personnel vanished through the call-up, and barely a third of the technicians remained. Studio premises were occupied by Government requisition. In 1939 there had been 22 studios using 65 sound stages. In 1942 there were only 9 studios using 30 sound stages. The Quota Act was maintained, however, and British cinemas were required to devote about one-seventh of their screen time to British films, the rest being occupied by the foreign product of Hollywood. The Quota had been for most exhibitors a legal bugbear before the War, since so few British films had been worth their playing time. Gradually, however, both the exhibitors and the public came to recognise the outstanding quality of many of the newer films. The Quota obligation remained a difficulty only because there were insufficient British films available to fulfil it, and re-issues of older films had to be played. Production dropped from 225 feature films in 1937 and 116 in 1938 to 56 in 1940, 56 again in 1941 and 60 in 1942. This remained the approximate annual output until 1946.

Inside the studios there developed a new craft of improvisation. Sets were built out of salvage wood, packing materials, hessian and plaster. Equipment due for scrapping was kept working by expert servicing. Coupon allocations had to be extracted from the Board of Trade for costumes. Bombs fell in or near the studios and set back productions. Carpenters and joiners, plasterers and decorators, electricians and engineers were needed for other work. Against all these difficulties and in the fulfilment of the innumerable regulations of war-time, the new cinema of Britain triumphed. A challenge to craftsmanship and technical ingenuity had to be met.

The industry also underwent considerable financial adjustment. Approximately half the studio space came under the ownership of the Rank Organisation, which by 1941 had acquired the two great theatre circuits, Odeon and Gaumont-British, representing over 600 important cinemas. Gradually most, though not all, of the finest directors and artists came to work within the studio-orbit of the Organisation, though they retained, as we shall see later, considerable production initiative. The strength of British cinema lies in this individuality of approach, no two studios producing the same type of films. The growing power of the Rank Organisation and its approach towards a monopolistic hold on the assets of British film resources have met with stern criticism both within and without the film world itself. The position of the few independent producers left is rendered precarious since they must obtain a circuit booking for every film they make to ensure their production costs, and the Rank Organisation owns two of the three great national circuits. Nevertheless, within the Organisation itself producers as different as Michael Powell and Gabriel Pascal, Sydney Box and Michael Balcon are making their films.

The vitality of technique shown by the young directors is one of the characteristics of the renaissance of British film art. Another is the sincerity with which human values are handled, and the authenticity of situation and environment in which these values are evolved. The future of the British film depends on its freedom from interference by interests which disregard these essential qualities.

The War Film

It is inevitable that the effects of a major catastrophe like the World War should transform the common material of every popular medium of expression. The mask was off, and a mythical mid-European state need no longer be used in the melodramas of espionage. Yet popular behaviour in this new war showed little desire for heroics or national self-display. Public speeches were for the most part toned down to expressions of solidarity and determination. When eventually the real war subjects began to be produced as distinct from the melodramas such as *Neutral Port*, this quiet sense of national feeling, this reticence and wry humour became part of the tradition which was to guide the conception of the remarkable films of 1942-45. The influence of this style of war film even spread to Hollywood, where a few, though by no means all, of their films revealed a calm confidence rather than a flamboyant gesture (for example *Guadalcanal Diary* and *The Story of G.I. Joe*). The British people went about the war as a difficult task to be worked off as efficiently as possible, and actions of unusual endurance or exceptional bravery were carried out as part of a routine. This desire for understatement developed as a regular attitude in the Services, and was faithfully put in the films by screen-writers, directors and actors only too conscious of the emotional implications and the wider national significance of the stories they were representing.

All violent action is in itself dramatic: its realistic portrayal will rouse strong emotions in an audience. With the official documentaries

84

and newsreels showing so much of the day to day violence of warfare the purpose of the feature films dealing with war themes was clearly to show the influence of this violence upon the individual. Everyone knew something of war through the common experience of sons and daughters, husbands and lovers. Almost everyone knew the sound of bombing and the vivid state of tension before the crash of explosion. The film producers were dealing with a psychologically aware audience. They could not afford, even if they had wished to do so, to turn into melodrama stories so close to the heart of Britain. Care was taken therefore to make the reconstruction of warfare on land, sea or in the air accurate to the conditions involved rather than spectacular for its own sake.

These stories of war dwelt on personal issues of comradeship, bravery, fear, tension, endurance, skill, boredom and hard work. The actors and actresses had to learn to combine the natural charm expected of screen personalities with great fidelity to the service people they were portraying. The personal always had to be merged into the general: the story into the common mass of experience. Sometimes the personal element seemed to overbalance too much as in Noel Coward's important film *In Which We Serve*: the result was considerable criticism by the public of a picture everyone was prepared to praise as a remarkable achievement in the period when the war film was discovering its technique. For the most part films such as *Millions Like Us, San Demetrio London, Nine Men, The Way Ahead, Waterloo Road* and *The Way to the Stars* resolved the personal equation, and showed us people in whom we could believe and whose experience was as genuine as our own. The war film discovered the common denominator of the British people.

It was natural therefore that the stories of these films grew out of direct war experience. *San Demetrio London* recreated a remarkable but true event in the experience of a group of merchant seamen. *The Foreman went to France* was an actual undertaking by a British foreman caught in the invasion of France. *Millions Like Us, The Gentle Sex, We Dive at Dawn* and *The Way to the Stars* are typical of stories created directly from war experience for the screen, not adapted in the usual way from books or plays. *Next of Kin* and *The*

Way Ahead were officially sponsored films made in the first place for audiences of the very men whom their stories concerned. The Royal Air Force itself turned feature-film producer and a team of service personnel made the remarkably authentic film *Journey Together* based on their own experiences. The Service Departments and the Ministry of Information encouraged the film industry by offering generous facilities and technical advice without which none of these films could have been made at all. It was a demonstration of the new spirit in the film industry and also of the new spirit in the public relations branches of the Service Departments.

It is commonly stated that the British documentary film influenced the style of the fiction film of the War. Documentary was a direct outcome of the development of public relations, or the function of explanation of the work of Government departments, industrial undertakings and all types of social organisation to the people whom they served. Documentary also revealed the importance of the service of the individual to the community. It was not concerned with fiction or the presentation of character for its own sake, and the successors to *North Sea*, where a very slight personal interest is developed in certain individuals, are the feature-length documentaries of the war-time Crown Film Unit like *Target for To-night* and *Western Approaches*, where the group still remains the dominant interest compared with any individuals in it. In *San Demetrio London* the approach is that of fiction, not documentary: the characters are all important in themselves. The audience-reaction to *Western Approaches* remains the reaction sought by documentary, that is the realisation of the service to the community which the merchant seamen undertook as shown by a typical event in their dangerous lives. The audience-reaction to *San Demetrio London* is sympathy and admiration for a number of individual men who make up part of the crew of a tanker and whom we come to know intimately as human beings. This is the more personal and emotional approach of fiction, and in no way destroys the authenticity of the background of the film or the value of its tribute to the merchant service. The film is an accommodating medium like literature: there is room for many ways of approach to the raw materials of life. This explains why the Crown Film Unit could

86

employ merchant seamen for *Western Approaches* whilst *San Demetrio London* could not have been made without actors.

The production of these films divides into three periods, the early period 1940-41, the middle period 1942-43, and the late period 1944-45. The early period did not produce a school of British cinema created by many directors: it covers the films of a few directors working individually. Michael Powell turned from a well-made story of espionage, *Contraband*, to the very individual story of the stranded group of Nazis at large in democratic Canada called *49th Parallel*, a film partly sponsored by the Government. It was a film which stressed personal relations rather than warfare, the clash of people living according to different philosophies. Carol Reed's *Gestapo* remained good melodrama for all its realistic touches. So did Asquith's *Freedom Radio* and Leslie Howard's *Pimpernel Smith*. The realistic approach to the experience of war began to appear in Pen Tennyson's *Convoy* and Maurice Elvey's *For Freedom*, with its story of the *Graf Spee*, the *Exeter* and the *Ajax*.

The second period 1942-43 established the maturity of the war film with *The Big Blockade* (Charles Frend), *The Foreman Went to France* (Charles Frend), *One of Our Aircraft is Missing* (Michael Powell), *Next of Kin* (Thorold Dickinson), *The First of the Few* (Leslie Howard), and *In Which We Serve* (Noel Coward and David Lean). Films dealing with occupied Europe showed attempts at greater authenticity in *The Day Will Dawn* (Harold French) and *To-morrow We Live* (George King). In 1943 the reputation of the war film was consolidated by the production of *Nine Men* (Harry Watt), *The Gentle Sex* (Leslie Howard), *We Dive at Dawn* (Anthony Asquith), *The Lamp Still Burns* (Maurice Elvey), *Millions Like Us* (Frank Launder and Sidney Gilliat) and *San Demetrio London* (Charles Frend). The films dealing with occupied Europe were *The Silver Fleet* (Vernon Sewell and Gordon Wellesley) and the short film made in Wales reconstructing the martyrdom of the Czech village Lidice, *The Silent Village* (Humphrey Jennings). In 1944 only two films appeared dealing directly with the War, *For Those in Peril* (Charles Crichton) and *The Way Ahead* (Carol Reed). It was evident that the peak period of production had passed with 1943, and the sense of emotional need for war subjects in our audiences was ended.

The late period 1944-45 represents therefore a change of approach in the war film. Among the chief films are *The Way Ahead*, made initially for the Army itself and *Journey Together* (John Boulting), another special case since it was made by the R.A.F. itself rather too late and in the style belonging to the middle period. The new approach was rather that of *The Way to the Stars* (Anthony Asquith) and *Waterloo Road* (Sidney Gilliat). From both of these films war scenes were excluded: the emphasis was wholly on the experiences of the individuals, and the impact of the war on their private lives and emotions. This is also true of the less effective because more 'star-dressed' and specifically box-office films, *I Live in Grosvenor Square* (Herbert Wilcox) and *Perfect Strangers* (Alexander Korda). The last brings us back full circle to an almost pre-war conception of war as a phenomenon in the plot of a romantic comedy.

The future of the British war film lies probably in the direction of narratives emphasising personal reactions, and produced with highly individual techniques. We cannot escape the impact of the war on the life of Britain and her people. We should not wish to do so. Authenticity will depend more on psychological accuracy than on realism of background, on the emotional understanding of human beings changed by participation in the varied experiences of war. The facilities for making pictures showing the details of war's phenomena have already passed. What is left is a changed people, and people are the stuff out of which the stories of good feature films are made.

The Individuality of British Studios

Considering the enormous output of Hollywood it has curiously little individuality of style and theme apart from the work of a very few notable directors. Films are made to certain patterns of entertainment value which have proved their worth at the box-offices of the world's cinemas. On the other hand, with a present output of less than a fifth of that of Hollywood there is far greater range of theme and style in the work of the new British studios. Many of these are dependent on the studio space and distribution channels controlled by the Rank Organisation, but they retain their own identity as far as their product is concerned.

It is important to realise that the best in British cinema is new. Its past is forgotten, or almost forgotten, though several producers and directors like Michael Balcon, Anthony Asquith and Michael Powell were contributors to what was good in pre-war British film art. Several of the directors of to-day are young men who were editors before the war (like Charles Frend, David Lean and Charles Crichton) or writers (like Frank Launder and Sidney Gilliat). Some, like Sydney Box, Cavalcanti and Harry Watt, have come over from work in documentary. Working with their own units or in studios with an enlightened production policy, the best British directors make each new film an experiment, a development of their own contribution to the art of the cinema.

This individuality covers all aspects of production, art direction, music and the use of colour. With only four Technicolor camera units at their disposal documentary and feature films as varied in colour style as *Western Approaches* and *Blithe Spirit*, *Henry V* and *This Happy Breed*, have been made. Colour is used not as a further chance for competitive display, but as an integral part of the interpretation of the story. It can be used with the extraordinary reticence of *This Happy Breed* where it so enhanced the realistic impression of the film that it was barely noticed at all: the audience was merely aware of a greater sense of actuality in what it was seeing. Colour was used for humour in the green and ghostly presence of Kay Hammond in *Blithe Spirit*, for temperature indication as well as dramatic effect in the documentary film *Steel*, for enhancing the sense of cold and isolation with the steely tones of the sea wastes in *Western Approaches*, and for developing the formal pageantry of set and costume in *Henry V*. The sense of colour-possibilities in directors and art directors is only just developing and is often far in advance of that of the process-technicians who still want to display the virtuosity of their particular colour system by loading every shot with as many colours as the process will carry. Except when colour is required for startling dramatic effects, its best use is that which is least noticeable. Its very presence greatly increases the quality and interest of a picture, as well as its range and depth. Though monochrome has many unique

89

and beautiful qualities of its own which justify its continuance in the future, its range is limited compared with the possibilities of colour, so circumscribed now by shortage of Technicolor camera units and lack of availability of the other processes with their different colour values.

A few films made before the War showed what opportunities were being missed by not setting more of our pictures in the British countryside. Notable films like *The Turn of the Tide, The Edge of the World* and *Man of Aran*, made by Flaherty on the Irish islands of Aran, were exceptional in taking the unit far away from the studios. Directors during and since the War have braved the climate and begun to show the many landscapes which this small island possesses in astonishing variety. Cornwall, Devon, the Lakes, the Scottish isles, Kent, Yorkshire, the Cotswolds, Wiltshire, the industrial Midlands, London and many other areas have appeared as settings for film stories. The variety of the scenery is matched by the variety of the weather, which, although it leads to delays unknown in the perpetual sunlight of California, gives cameramen chances of capturing an endless variety of lighting and cloud effects. As far as studio-sets are concerned, improvisation and ingenuity have disguised the lack of raw materials, while the sets for films like *Henry V* and *Caesar and Cleopatra* have been as lavish as any known on the screen. Lighting, which is a branch of camera-work, has greatly enhanced the beautiful sets used by Gainsborough studios in films like *The Man in Grey* and the reconstructions of Rex Whistler's designs for *A Place of One's Own*. Plaster-work in British film sets is often as beautiful as it is skilfully executed. The period settings were outstanding in these films and also in *Gaslight, Kipps, The Prime Minister, The Young Mr. Pitt, Champagne Charlie* and *Fanny by Gaslight*. Most of these sets have been realistic in design, the lighting and camera-work emphasising and enhancing compositional values. In *Henry V*, however, experiments were made with formal settings, which beautiful in themselves and unrealistic as Shakespeare's verse, did not match easily with such scenes as the battle of Agincourt, which had to be shot in the open fields of Ireland. Because the film is a photographic medium and therefore normally associated with the reproduction of reality, it does

90

not mean that fantasy cannot be introduced, provided it is used with a subtle appreciation of its powers in an art which excels in creating the illusion of actuality.

Another notable feature of recent British films has been their music. Special scores have been composed by distinguished musicians like William Walton, Benjamin Britten, William Alwyn, Clifton Parker, Vaughan Williams and Arthur Bliss for both documentary and feature films. Classical music of the highest order has been extensively introduced, often with very satisfactory results as in Sydney Box's *The Seventh Veil*. Muir Mathieson and the London Symphony Orchestra have in innumerable pictures set standards of execution which are of the greatest importance to the future of music in British films. An original score, however, is in the last analysis the only proper one for a film making full use of musical associations with the visual image: well-known classical music may well create responses or sensations which overbalance the emotional values of the film itself.

In the end all films of artistic importance have a style deriving from the quality of the visual imagination of the director and his unit, and from the pace with which they are scripted and edited. The pace varies with the director and the subject; it is often a quality of temperament. The Gilliat-Launder films tend to move fast, whereas most British films on the whole tend to move slowly. They frequently suffer from over-scripting and are in danger of allowing the dialogue to kill the pace. Pace is the lifeblood of a film's tempo, its vitality of movement. The qualities which are uppermost in our cinema are humanity of characterisation (a quality shared with the French, and very national in its observation and choice of actors and actresses) and a growing ability to create a cinematic poetry peculiar to British films, as indeed it must be to each national creative art. This poetry is the sign of a nation's artistic maturity. It occurs when dialogue, acting, photography and the movement of sound and image merge to create a deep emotional impression. It cannot, of course, be defined. It can only be recognised and acknowledged. It is to be found in moments of *In Which We Serve, The First of the Few, The Gentle Sex, Millions Like Us, San Demetrio London, The Way Ahead* and especially *The Way to the Stars*. These are war films: it is also present in

91

films like *The Stars Look Down, The Proud Valley, Love on the Dole, This Happy Breed, I Know Where I'm Going,* and especially *Brief Encounter.* An emotional situation is in itself not enough: there are emotional situations in all films. Poetry arises when the emotions portrayed are of a universal quality and application. It arises when writer, director, actor and cameraman join their skills together to realise on the screen the imaginative projection of the emotions. It is then that the poetry of cinema is born, a poetry which has been created collectively by all the great film-producing countries in their finest work. Our studios have now succeeded in adding the British feature film to the vanguard of this new and developing art of the cinema.

The General Feature Film

By 1944 public desire was waning for film stories resolving the emotional problems and values raised by the War. Producers, working always a year or more ahead, had to plan films which would form a more permanent basis for entertainment in the future conditions of peace. The Rank Organisation prepared for an extension of British film exhibition overseas so that more ambitious programmes could be planned than the home market alone would allow. In this spirit the spectacular films *Henry V* and *Caesar and Cleopatra* together costing nearly two million pounds and each taking two years to produce, challenged the large-scale productions of Hollywood. The normal British feature film costs now between one and two hundred thousand pounds to make, whilst those in colour cost around a quarter of a million pounds. The British market alone can gross some £300,000 for a film which is very successful at the box-office. Most films, therefore, are made for less than £150,000 and though they will play to a profit in Britain, they are often produced to satisfy potential audiences overseas as well. The Rank Organisation has acquired theatres in the Dominions and in foreign countries, including America, to act as exhibition centres for British films, and negotiations have been completed with a number of American distributors for British films to be handled along with the productions of Hollywood in America and South America.

92

The more important of the general feature films have therefore been produced during and since 1944, when the War began to turn towards its last major phase. The desire for more serious themes had, however, led to the production even before the War began of two films set in the mining areas of the north of England and South Wales, *The Stars Look Down* (Carol Reed) and *The Proud Valley* (Pen Tennyson), and in 1940 Roy and John Boulting finished *Pastor Hall* adapted from Ernst Toller's play based on the experiences of Pastor Niemoller. In 1941 John Baxter's two social films *Love on the Dole* and *The Common Touch* dealt with the human problems of unemployment and vagrancy, and Pascal made *Major Barbara* from Bernard Shaw's play. In 1942 appeared the Boultings' adaptation of Robert Ardrey's fantasy on the struggle for social progress, *Thunder Rock*. On the lighter side from the point of view of entertainment values were Carol Reed's admirable *Kipps*, and two melodramas, one directed by Thorold Dickinson, *Gaslight*, and the other by Anthony Asquith, *Cottage to Let*. Two notable historical films, the first about the life of Disraeli, *The Prime Minister* (Thorold Dickinson), and the second, *The Young Mr. Pitt* (Carol Reed), were outstanding. Released in 1943, Anthony Asquith's *Demi-Paradise* and Michael Powell's *The Life and Death of Colonel Blimp* were both unusual films of the type which helped to widen the range of subject and treatment which it has been said before is characteristic of the variety of recent British films, whilst Rodney Ackland's *Thursday's Child* was an excellent satire on the family difficulties of a child film star. The series of romantic costume pictures now associated with Gainsborough Studios started notably with *The Man in Grey*.

Here, then, produced in the worst days of violence and austerity, were over a dozen pictures which helped to launch the new movement for films of a high quality outside those specifically dealing with the War itself. In 1944 the number increased in proportion to the decrease of the war films. John Baxter's *Shipbuilders* was a serious study of the human problems of the Clyde shipyards, but a much lighter or a more romantic spirit was beginning to enter the themes of the newer films like Ealing Studios' *Champagne Charlie* and *The Halfway House*, Bernard Miles' *The Tawny Pipit* and Michael Powell's *A Canterbury*

Tale. The popularity of *This Happy Breed* (Noel Coward and David Lean) showed that the British public were prepared to see themselves on the screen as well as the stars of an unapproachable dream-world. Anthony Asquith's *Fanny by Gaslight* was a remarkable period picture, and *They Came to a City* a further sign of experiment, though as a filmed version of J. B. Priestley's discussion-play it did not make good cinema. The year ended with Laurence Olivier's production of Shakespeare's *Henry V*: this was a magnificent achievement with many sequences which made cinema of Shakespeare (the description of the death of Falstaff, the night before Agincourt in the French camp, Henry himself talking with his soldiers by the camp fire and the sequence of the battle shot in Ireland). For the most part, however, this film could not make full use of the resources of the cinema since it was bound to the verbal wheel of Shakespeare's text written for a rhetorical theatre. The camera therefore had to record rather than take charge of the greater part of this most distinguished and beautifully mounted production.

In 1945 *Strawberry Roan* (Maurice Elvey) showed us Wiltshire on the screen, *Johnny Frenchman* (Charles Frend) was filmed in Cornwall, whilst *I Know Where I'm Going* (Michael Powell) used the magnificent scenery of the Scottish Isles. *Painted Boats* (Charles Crichton) was a beautiful short film of barge-life in the industrial Midlands of Britain. The period films, *Pink String and Sealing Wax* (Robert Hamer) and *A Place of One's Own* (Bernard Knowles) showed again that this branch of British cinema is of permanent value when the atmosphere of period is imaginatively recreated. *Blithe Spirit* (Noel Coward and David Lean) was good entertainment and interesting for its use of colour, but was of less importance cinematically than the same unit's *Brief Encounter*, the most perfectly written, acted and directed film of the year: the symbolic use of the station and trains was a fine example of the power of the cinema to make background a significant part of the emotional structure of a film. Sydney Box's first production from Riverside Studios, *The Seventh Veil*, with its use of classical music in a romantic story of the career of a concert pianist, was a demonstration of what can be produced in a short time at a comparatively low expenditure. It was a fine box-office picture with dignity of treatment and a beautiful performance by Ann Todd as the pianist. Ealing Studios' melodrama of the supernatural, *Dead of Night*, was the most ingenious film of the year. *Caesar and Cleopatra* was the most elaborately spectacular. Even more than *Henry V*, and in spite of the excellent acting of Vivien Leigh and Claude Rains, it suffered from being bound to a dramatic text intended for the theatre and lacking therefore the intimacy of speech and continual allowance for details of reaction, which it is the cinema's special technique to convey. *The Rake's Progress*, the first film from Frank Launder's and Sidney Gilliat's Individual Pictures, achieved a pace which most British pictures lack, and was as much a subtle political and social satire as a romantic story.

This brief record of selected pictures is enough to demonstrate the vitality and variety of contemporary British films. They have, along with the important war pictures, consolidated the reputations of stars well established before 1939, such as David Niven, Vivien Leigh, Laurence Olivier, Ralph Richardson, Ann Todd, Flora Robson, Robert Donat, Eric Portman and Rex Harrison. They have given star rank to significant actors and actresses like John Mills, Michael Redgrave, Robert Newton, Roger Livesey, John Clements, Bernard Miles, Mervyn Johns, Richard Attenborough, Phyllis Calvert, Celia Johnson, Rosamund John, Googie Withers, Lilli Palmer and Sheila Sim, whilst stars like James Mason, Stewart Granger and Margaret Lockwood are as popular at the British box-office as the most famous American players. The old prejudice against British pictures has almost completely disappeared, though a bad reputation in entertainment dies hard with the greater public.

It remains now to maintain and develop the quality of British films. Our greatest entertainment industry selling nearly thirty million seats a week exhibits an American programme four-fifths of the time. It is necessary therefore to use ingenuity to solve the problems of shortage of equipment and studio space. It is necessary to make films of good quality more quickly so that more will be available to exhibitors to help redress the proportion of British to American pictures now being shown. Above all it is necessary to train more technicians and artists of integrity so that with the increase in film

95

production standards will also be maintained. This alone can save us from becoming once more a resting-place for Hollywood personnel looking for contracts, or from producing quantities of third-rate films by second-rate technicians. Quality alone can save us from losing to America the many good actors and actresses we have discovered and will continue to discover if all goes well. British films must retain their national integrity without becoming merely insular: they must be honestly British without being dull as entertainment. The best cinema of other countries has been able to contribute a national art to motion pictures. Having taken our place alongside them we must continue to make pictures which justify the claim that the film is the most progressive popular art of the twentieth century.

THE STARS LOOK DOWN
Grafton Films, 1939. Carol Reed

G

GASLIGHT
British National
1940
Thorold Dickinson

THE PROUD
VALLEY
Ealing Studios
1940
Pen Tennyson

PASTOR HALL
Charter Films, 1940. Roy Boulting

G*

THE PRIME
MINISTER
Warner British
1941
Thorold Dickinson

KIPPS
20th Cent. Fox
British
1941
Carol Reed

THUNDER ROCK
Charter Films
1942
Roy Boulting

PIMPERNEL SMITH
British National
1941
Leslie Howard

THE FOREMAN WENT TO FRANCE
Ealing Studios, 1942. Charles Frend

IN WHICH WE
SERVE
Two Cities, 1942
Noel Coward and
David Lean

ONE OF OUR
AIRCRAFT IS
MISSING
British National
1942
Michael Powell

NEXT OF KIN
Ealing Studios
1942
Thorold Dickinson

THE YOUNG
MR. PITT
20th Cent. Fox
British, 1942
Carol Reed

THURSDAY'S CHILD
A.B.P.C.
1943
Rodney Ackland

THE MAN IN GREY
Gainsborough
1943
Leslie Arliss

NINE MEN
Ealing Studios
1943
Harry Watt

THE WAY AHEAD
Two Cities
1944
Carol Reed

CHAMPAGNE
CHARLIE
Ealing Studios
1944
Alberto Cavalcanti

FANNY BY
GASLIGHT
Gainsborough
1944
Anthony Asquith

TAWNY PIPIT
Two Cities
1944
Charles Saunders
and Bernard Miles

A CANTERBURY
TALE
Archers
Productions
1944
Michael Powell

THIS HAPPY
BREED
Two Cities
1944
David Lean

FIDDLERS THREE
Ealing Studios
1944
Harry Watt

THEY CAME TO A
CITY
Ealing Studios
1944
Basil Dearden

HENRY V
Two Cities
1944
Laurence Olivier

PINK STRING AND
SEALING WAX
Ealing Studios
1945
Robert Hamer

DEAD OF NIGHT
Ealing Studios
1945
Cavalcanti,
Crichton, Dearden,
Hamer

THE WAY TO THE
STARS
Two Cities
1945
Anthony Asquith

BRIEF ENCOUNTER
Cineguild
1945
David Lean

WATERLOO ROAD
Gainsborough
1945
Sidney Gilliat

JOURNEY
TOGETHER
R.A.F. Film Unit
1945
John Boulting

I KNOW WHERE
I'M GOING
Archers
Productions
1945
Michael Powell

PAINTED BOATS
Ealing Studios
1945
Charles Crichton

The Arno Press Cinema Program

THE LITERATURE OF CINEMA

Series I & II

American Academy of Political and Social Science. **The Motion Picture in Its Economic and Social Aspects,** edited by Clyde L. King. **The Motion Picture Industry,** edited by Gordon S. Watkins. *The Annals,* November, 1926/1927.

Agate, James. **Around Cinemas.** 1946.

Agate, James. **Around Cinemas.** (Second Series). 1948.

Balcon, Michael, Ernest Lindgren, Forsyth Hardy and Roger Manvell. **Twenty Years of British Film, 1925-1945.** 1947.

Bardèche, Maurice and Robert Brasillach. **The History of Motion Pictures,** edited by Iris Barry. 1938.

Benoit-Levy, Jean. **The Art of the Motion Picture.** 1946.

Blumer, Herbert. **Movies and Conduct.** 1933.

Blumer, Herbert and Philip M. Hauser. **Movies, Delinquency, and Crime.** 1933.

Buckle, Gerard Fort. **The Mind and the Film.** 1926.

Carter, Huntly. **The New Spirit in the Cinema.** 1930.

Carter, Huntly. **The New Spirit in the Russian Theatre, 1917-1928.** 1929.

Carter, Huntly. **The New Theatre and Cinema of Soviet Russia.** 1924.

Charters, W. W. **Motion Pictures and Youth.** 1933.

Cinema Commission of Inquiry. **The Cinema: Its Present Position and Future Possibilities.** 1917.

Dale, Edgar. **The Content of Motion Pictures.** 1935.

Dale, Edgar. **How to Appreciate Motion Pictures.** 1937.

Dale, Edgar. **Children's Attendance at Motion Pictures.** Dysinger, Wendell S. and Christian A. Ruckmick. **The Emotional Responses of Children to the Motion Picture Situation.** 1935.

Dale, Edgar, Fannie W. Dunn, Charles F. Hoban, Jr., and Etta Schneider. **Motion Pictures in Education: A Summary of the Literature.** 1938.

Davy, Charles. **Footnotes to the Film.** 1938.

Dickinson, Thorold and Catherine De la Roche. **Soviet Cinema.** 1948.

Dickson, W. K. L., and Antonia Dickson. **History of the Kinetograph, Kinetoscope and Kinetophonograph.** 1895.

Forman, Henry James. **Our Movie Made Children.** 1935.

Freeburg, Victor Oscar. **The Art of Photoplay Making.** 1918.

Freeburg, Victor Oscar. **Pictorial Beauty on the Screen.** 1923.

Hall, Hal, editor. **Cinematographic Annual,** 2 vols. 1930/1931.

Hampton, Benjamin B. **A History of the Movies.** 1931.

Hardy, Forsyth. **Scandinavian Film.** 1952.

Hepworth, Cecil M. **Animated Photography: The A B C of the Cinematograph.** 1900.

Hoban, Charles F., Jr., and Edward B. Van Ormer. **Instructional Film Research 1918-1950.** 1950.

Holaday, Perry W. and George D. Stoddard. **Getting Ideas from the Movies.** 1933.

Hopwood, Henry V. **Living Pictures.** 1899.

Hulfish, David S. **Motion-Picture Work.** 1915.

Hunter, William. **Scrutiny of Cinema.** 1932.

Huntley, John. **British Film Music.** 1948.

Irwin, Will. **The House That Shadows Built.** 1928.

Jarratt, Vernon. **The Italian Cinema.** 1951.

Jenkins, C. Francis. **Animated Pictures.** 1898.

Lang, Edith and George West. **Musical Accompaniment of Moving Pictures.** 1920.

L'Art Cinematographique, Nos. 1-8. 1926-1931.

London, Kurt. **Film Music.** 1936.

Lutz, E[dwin] G[eorge]. **The Motion-Picture Cameraman.** 1927.

Manvell, Roger. **Experiment in the Film.** 1949.

Marey, Etienne Jules. **Movement.** 1895.

Martin, Olga J. **Hollywood's Movie Commandments.** 1937.

Mayer, J. P. **Sociology of Film: Studies and Documents.** 1946. New Introduction by J. P. Mayer.

Münsterberg, Hugo. **The Photoplay: A Psychological Study.** 1916.

Nicoll, Allardyce. **Film and Theatre.** 1936.

Noble, Peter. **The Negro in Films.** 1949.

Peters, Charles C. **Motion Pictures and Standards of Morality.** 1933.

Peterson, Ruth C. and L. L. Thurstone. **Motion Pictures and the Social Attitudes of Children.** Shuttleworth, Frank K. and Mark A. May. **The Social Conduct and Attitudes of Movie Fans.** 1933.

Phillips, Henry Albert. **The Photodrama.** 1914.

Photoplay Research Society. **Opportunities in the Motion Picture Industry.** 1922.

Rapée, Erno. **Encyclopaedia of Music for Pictures.** 1925.

Rapée, Erno. **Motion Picture Moods for Pianists and Organists.** 1924.

Renshaw, Samuel, Vernon L. Miller and Dorothy P. Marquis. **Children's Sleep.** 1933.

Rosten, Leo C. **Hollywood: The Movie Colony, The Movie Makers.** 1941.

Sadoul, Georges. **French Film.** 1953.

Screen Monographs I, 1923-1937. 1970.

Screen Monographs II, 1915-1930. 1970.

Sinclair, Upton. **Upton Sinclair Presents William Fox.** 1933.

Talbot, Frederick A. **Moving Pictures.** 1912.

Thorp, Margaret Farrand. **America at the Movies.** 1939.

Wollenberg, H. H. **Fifty Years of German Film.** 1948.

RELATED BOOKS AND PERIODICALS

Allister, Ray. **Friese-Greene: Close-Up of an Inventor.** 1948.

Art in Cinema: A Symposium of the Avant-Garde Film, edited by Frank Stauffacher. 1947.

The Art of Cinema: Selected Essays. New Foreword by George Amberg. 1971.

Balázs, Béla. **Theory of the Film.** 1952.

Barry, Iris. **Let's Go to the Movies.** 1926.

de Beauvoir, Simone. **Brigitte Bardot and the Lolita Syndrome.** 1960.

Carrick, Edward. **Art and Design in the British Film.** 1948.

Close Up. Vols. 1-10, 1927-1933 (all published).

Cogley, John. **Report on Blacklisting. Part I: The Movies.** 1956.

Eisenstein, S. M. **Que Viva Mexico!** 1951.

Experimental Cinema. 1930-1934 (all published).

Feldman, Joseph and Harry. **Dynamics of the Film.** 1952.

Film Daily Yearbook of Motion Pictures. Microfilm, 18 reels,
    35 mm. 1918-1969.

Film Daily Yearbook of Motion Pictures. 1970.

Film Daily Yearbook of Motion Pictures. (Wid's Year Book).
    3 vols., 1918-1922.

The Film Index: A Bibliography. Vol. I: The Film as Art. 1941.

Film Society Programmes. 1925-1939 (all published).

Films: A Quarterly of Discussion and Analysis. Nos. 1-4, 1939-1940
    (all published).

Flaherty, Frances Hubbard. **The Odyssey of a Film-Maker:
    Robert Flaherty's Story.** 1960.

General Bibliography of Motion Pictures, edited by Carl Vincent,
    Riccardo Redi, and Franco Venturini. 1953.

Hendricks, Gordon. **Origins of the American Film.** 1961-1966. New
    Introduction by Gordon Hendricks.

Hound and Horn: Essays on Cinema, 1928-1934. 1971.

Huff, Theodore. **Charlie Chaplin.** 1951.

Kahn, Gordon. **Hollywood on Trial.** 1948.

New York Times Film Reviews, 1913-1968. 1970.

Noble, Peter. **Hollywood Scapegoat: The Biography of Erich
    von Stroheim.** 1950.

Robson, E. W. and M. M. **The Film Answers Back.** 1939.

Weinberg, Herman G., editor. **Greed.** 1971.

Wollenberg, H. H. **Anatomy of the Film.** 1947.

Wright, Basil. **The Use of the Film.** 1948.